D1488365

NOTRE DAME

DAILY DEVOTIONS FOR DIE-HARD FANS

FIGHTING IRISH

NOTRE DAME

Daily Devotions for Die-Hard Fans: Notre Dame Fighting Irish
© 2016 Ed McMinn
Extra Point Publishers; P.O. Box 871; Perry GA 31069

All rights reserved, including the right to reproduce this book or portions thereof in any form whatsoever.
Manufactured in the United States of America.

Unless otherwise noted, scripture quotations are taken from the *Holy Bible, New International Version.* Copyright © 1973, 1978, 1984, by the International Bible Society. Used by permission of Zondervan.

Cover design by John Powell and Slynn McMinn
Interior design by Slynn McMinn

Visit us at www.die-hardfans.com.

Every effort has been made to identify copyright holders. Any omissions are unintentional. Extra Point Publishers should be notified in writing immediately for full acknowledgement in future editions.

FIGHTING IRISH

Daily Devotions for Die-Hard Fans
Available Titles

ACC
Clemson Tigers
Duke Blue Devils
FSU Seminoles
Georgia Tech Yellow Jackets
North Carolina Tar Heels
NC State Wolfpack
Notre Dame Fighting Irish
Virginia Cavaliers
Virginia Tech Hokies

BIG 10
Michigan Wolverines
Nebraska Cornhuskers
Ohio State Buckeyes
Penn State Nittany Lions

BIG 12
Baylor Bears
Oklahoma Sooners
Oklahoma State Cowboys
TCU Horned Frogs
Texas Longhorns
Texas Tech Red Raiders

SEC
Alabama Crimson Tide
MORE Alabama Crimson Tide
Arkansas Razorbacks
Auburn Tigers
MORE Auburn Tigers
Florida Gators
Georgia Bulldogs
MORE Georgia Bulldogs
Kentucky Wildcats
LSU Tigers
Mississippi State Bulldogs
Missouri Tigers
Ole Miss Rebels
South Carolina Gamecocks
MORE South Carolina Gamecocks
Texas A&M Aggies
Tennessee Volunteers

and *NASCAR*

Daily Devotions for Die-Hard Kids
Available Titles
Alabama, Auburn, Baylor, Georgia, Texas, Texas A&M

---

www.die-hardfans.com

NOTRE DAME

DAILY DEVOTIONS FOR DIE-HARD FANS

FIGHTING IRISH

IN THE BEGINNING

Read Genesis 1; 2:1-3.

"God saw all that he had made, and it was very good" (v. 1:31).

Notre Dame has the University of Michigan to thank for help in starting its football program.

In 1887, this new game appearing on college campuses had caught the attention of some Notre Dame students. Wanting to learn the game properly, they wrote to two Michigan students who had been at Notre Dame the year before, asking for help. The pair responded by suggesting that the Michigan football team travel to South Bend for a training session and a game.

The visit came on Nov. 23, the day before Thanksgiving. The Michigan players took the train and were driven by horse and carriage to the campus, some six miles from the station. They arrived early since they had to make a connection for a game in Chicago the next day. Thus, the first-ever Notre Dame football game was played in the morning. A school holiday was declared, and most of the student body turned out. The school band was on hand, as was a cheerleader.

The visiting students toured the campus for an hour or so before putting on their white uniforms and getting down to the business at hand. They first scrimmaged some with players from both schools on each team. After the Notre Dame boys had picked up the basics, they played a real game.

FIGHTING IRISH

Since it had to be finished by noon to allow time for lunch and the train connection, the game lasted only 30 minutes. Michigan scored two touchdowns on a muddy field for an 8-0 win.

After lunch, the Notre Dame president thanked the Michigan boys for their visit and declared that "a cordial reception would always await them at Notre Dame." The carriages were ready by one o'clock, and "amid the rousing cheers of Notre Dame students, the Michigan players departed."

Football at Notre Dame had begun.

Beginnings are important, but what we make of them is even more important. Consider, for example, how far the Notre Dame football program has come since that first season. Every morning, you get a gift from God: a new beginning. God hands to you, as an expression of divine love, a new day full of promise and the chance to right the wrongs in your life.

You can use the day to pay a debt, start a new relationship, replace a burned-out light bulb, tell your family you love them, chase a dream, solve a nagging problem . . . or not.

God simply provides the gift. How you use it is up to you. People often talk wistfully about starting over or making a new beginning. God gives you the chance with the dawning of every new day. You have the chance today to make things right — and that includes your relationship with God.

The game was interesting, and has started an enthusiastic football boom. It is hoped that coming years will witness a series of these contests.
— The Notre Dame Scholastic on the first-ever football game

Every day is not just a dawn;
it is a precious chance to start over or begin anew.

TOO LATE

Read Luke 16:19-31.

"'Let [Lazarus] warn them, so that they will not also come to this place of torment'" (v. 28b).

Stephon Tuitt was too late to take part in his first-ever weight-lifting session. He had a good excuse, though; he walked almost eleven miles to get there.

As a sophomore defensive end in 2012, Tuitt was a first-team All-American for the Irish team that finished the regular season undefeated. He turned pro after his junior season.

Tuitt's football exploits began when he uncharacteristically decided to disobey his mother. Concerned about his grades, she had expressly told the rising freshman he could not play football. "I really wanted to do it," he said. "I felt it in my heart." So he decided to walk to his high school, all 10.8 miles, and take part in the first workout of the spring.

Needless to say, mama was furious when she heard what her son had done, but when she saw how happy he was playing football, she relented. Tuitt still had to mind his chores at home, however. On several occasions when he failed to take care of business, she showed up at practice to "drag her giant son off the field and usher him into the car without giving him time to even remove his pads."

About that day Tuitt took a long hike. He showed up dripping sweat to discover the players had finished their workout and had left. Only coach Matt Fligg remained. He looked over the 6-3, 200-lb. freshman who would obviously grow some more and asked him where he'd been. Walking, was the answer. The stunned coach forgave him for being late and granted him a spot on the junior varsity.

Too late for the workout, Stephon Tuitt was just in time to begin a productive football career.

Perhaps the most terrifying scenario Jesus ever presented is the parable of Lazarus and the rich man. It relates the awful fate of those who come to understand Jesus' message too late.

The rich man's selfishness and not his wealth doomed him to Hell. By the time he realized what he had done, it was too late for him to be delivered from the agony he suffered. Too late did he lift his eyes toward Heaven.

We know he finally understood because he begged Abraham to send Lazarus to his family with a message that would deliver them from his awful fate. But it was too late for that, too. Instead, Abraham said, all the family members had to take the message of God's prophets to heart for themselves.

Where do we the saved fit into this parable? Is it possible that when we fail each day to speak of Jesus to an unsaved family member, friend, or co-worker, that we metaphorically pass them by just as the rich man did Lazarus? Where does that leave us when it's too late for those we might have witnessed to?

He took the long way.
   — *Stephon Tuitt's mother on why he was late for his first workout*

**It's not too late to speak of Jesus today
to someone who's unsaved.**

DOWNRIGHT CRAZY

Read Luke 13:31-35.

"Some Pharisees came to Jesus and said to him, 'Leave this place and go somewhere else. Herod wants to kill you.' He replied, 'Go tell that fox . . . I must keep going today and tomorrow and the next day'" (vv. 31-33).

Digger Phelps once wrote Ara Parseghian a letter that could kindly be described as downright crazy. The Notre Dame head football coach certainly thought so.

Phelps is the winningest men's basketball coach in Irish history. From 1971-1991, his teams won 393 games with twelve seasons of twenty or more wins. They had one stretch of six straight top-10 finishes. The 1978 team made the Final Four. In 2014, Phelps was inducted into Notre Dame's Ring of Honor.

All that lay in the future in 1965 when Phelps became the head boys basketball coach at St. Gabriel's High School in Hazelton, Penn. Even as he embarked on his coaching career, the 24-year-old had Notre Dame on his mind. He redesigned his team's uniforms and put a shamrock on the game pants. The area was so strong for the Irish that the nuns at the school said the rosary and lit candles for Notre Dame on football game days.

Phelps had grown up in New York a die-hard Notre Dame fan. "I loved the essence of Notre Dame and what the University stood for," he said. Prior to the 1965 season, though he had never even seen the campus, the unproven, untested first-year high-school coach wrote a letter to Parseghian telling him about his dream of becoming Notre Dame's men's basketball coach.

Six years later, in the spring of 1971, that dream came true. And what about that letter? When the new head coach went to his first Irish golf outing, Parseghian was there. Phelps told sports information director Roger Valdiserri about his letter, and he spoke to Parseghian about it. The head coach said he had a "crazy letter file" in his office. Sure enough, it was there. Valdiserri used that crazy letter in the press guide that fall.

What some see as crazy often is shrewd instead. Like the time you went into business for yourself or when you decided to go back to school. Maybe it was when you fixed up that old house. Or when you bought that new company's stock.

You know a good thing when you see it but are also shrewd enough to spot something that's downright crazy. Jesus was that way, too. He knew that his entering Jerusalem was in complete defiance of all apparent reason and logic since a whole bunch of folks who wanted to kill him were waiting for him there.

Nevertheless, he went because he also knew that when the great drama had played out he would defeat not only his personal enemies but the most fearsome enemy of all: death itself.

It was, after all, a shrewd move that provided the way to your salvation.

It does seem crazy today that I would write a letter to the football coach about becoming the basketball coach.

— *Digger Phelps*

It's so good it sounds crazy — but it's not: through faith in Jesus, you can have eternal life with God.

DAY 4

HOLLYWOOD ENDING

Read Luke 24:1-12.

"Why do you look for the living among the dead? He is not here; he has risen!" (vv. 5, 6a)

What Joe Montana and his teammates pulled off in the 1979 Cotton Bowl was pure Hollywood.

Despite a windchill of ten below zero and blizzard-like conditions on New Year's Day in Dallas, the Houston Cougars played well and romped to a 34-12 lead in the fourth quarter. Meanwhile, Montana, the team's senior quarterback, spent halftime shivering uncontrollably as he battled a below-normal body temperature. "We were told that Joe wasn't coming back in the second half and we thought it was over," said center Dave Huffman.

Hey, this is Hollywood. Enter some chicken soup.

After the second half began, team doctor Les Bodnar opened up a packet of chicken soup that he had received as a Christmas stocking stuffer from his daughter. He warmed the soup up and spoon-fed Montana until his temperature rose to normal.

Montana returned to the game late in the third quarter, but the Cougars kept on coasting, romping to that cozy 34-12 lead deep into the fourth quarter. Time to cue the Hollywood ending.

Tony Belden blocked a punt and Steve Cichy returned it 33 yards for a touchdown with 7:25 left. Montana hit halfback Vagas Ferguson for the two-point conversion. 34-20. Montana then led the Irish on a 61-yard drive, scoring himself from the 2 and finding receiver Kris Haines for the conversion. 34-28 with 4:15 left.

After Houston failed on fourth down, the Irish quickly moved to the Cougar 8 with two seconds left. In the huddle, Montana asked Haines if he could beat his man. When Haines said he could, Montana smiled and said, "Let's do it." They did; he found Haines in the corner of the end zone. Joe Unis then booted the PAT to complete a 23-point comeback in less than eight minutes.

35-34. Pure Hollywood.

The world tells us that happy endings are for fairy tales and the movies, that reality is Cinderella dying in childbirth and her prince getting killed in a peasant uprising. But that's just another of the world's lies.

The truth is that Jesus Christ has been producing happy endings for almost two millennia. That's because in Jesus lies the power to change and to rescue a life no matter how desperate the situation. Jesus is the master at putting shattered lives back together, of healing broken hearts and broken relationships, of resurrecting lost dreams.

And as for living happily ever after — God really means it. The greatest Hollywood ending of them all was written on a Sunday morning centuries ago when Jesus left a tomb and death behind. With faith in Jesus, your life can have that same ending. You live with God in peace, joy, and love — forever. The End.

When Joe came back to the field, I started thinking this was a fairy tale.
— Kris Haines

Hollywood's happy endings are products of imagination; the happy endings Jesus produces are real and are yours for the asking.

DAY 5

BAD ADVICE

Read Isaiah 9:2-7.

"And he will be called Wonderful Counselor" (v. 9:6b).

Once during a game, Bill Fischer got such bad advice from a teammate that it nearly cost him some grievous bodily harm.

As a senior in 1948, Fischer was the captain of the squad that came within a tie with Southern Cal of winning a third straight national title. Playing left guard, Fischer was All-America in 1947 and '48. He won the Outland Trophy in 1948 as the nation's best lineman.

Fischer avoided playing for Illinois only because a persuasive Irish coach happened upon him at a Chicago train station. The Illinois head coach had sent him a one-way ticket to Champaign, and in 1945 the recruit was at a station with the ticket in his hand. Fortunately for Irish football history, the train for South Bend left from the same station, and Irish assistant Gene Ronzani spotted Fischer. He talked the youngster into riding with him to the Notre Dame campus. That one trip was all it took.

While Fischer obviously benefited from what Ronzani had to say to him, he certainly regretted some advice he got in the 1945 Army game. With its ranks decimated by World War II, Notre Dame was no match for the West Point powerhouse. Army rolled to an easy 48-0 win. As Fischer put it, "They were pushing us all over the place." Along the way, tackle Jack Fallon suggested the rookie take a swing at the guy across the line from him.

Fischer did. After the play, the cadet grabbed him and snarled, "Look, fat boy, if you try that again, you're apt to get killed." Fischer heeded the warning, which was a good thing. The opponent he had punched was All-American tackle Tex Coulter, who was the academy's heavyweight boxing champion.

Like Bill Fischer, we all need a little advice now and then. More often than not, we turn to professional counselors, who are all over the place. Marriage counselors, grief counselors, guidance counselors in our schools, rehabilitation counselors, all sorts of mental health and addiction counselors — We even have pet counselors. No matter what our situation or problem, we can find plenty of advice for the taking.

The problem, of course, is that we find advice easy to offer but hard to take. We also have a rueful tendency to solicit the wrong source for advice, seeking counsel that doesn't really solve our problem but that instead enables us to continue with it.

Our need for outside advice, for an independent perspective on our situation, is actually God-given. God serves many functions in our lives, but one role clearly delineated in his Word is that of Counselor. Jesus himself is described as the "Wonderful Counselor." All the advice we need in our lives is right there for the asking; we don't even have to pay for it except with our faith. God is always there for us to listen, to lead, and to guide.

I have never regretted it one bit.
  — Bill Fischer on following Gene Ronzani's advice about Notre Dame

**We all need and seek advice in our lives,
but the ultimate and most wonderful Counselor
is of divine and not human origin.**

HOW DISAPPOINTING!

Read Ezra 3.

"Many of the older priests and Levites and family heads, who had seen the former temple, wept aloud when they saw the foundation of this temple being laid, while many others shouted for joy" (v. 12).

Raghib "Rocket" Ismail blew a touchdown on his first play in a Notre Dame uniform. He was obviously disappointed, but his head coach? Not really.

Ismail was a "one-of-a-kind talent," a two-time first-team All-America who finished second in the voting for the 1990 Heisman Trophy. He set a number of school records, including five kickoffs returned for touchdowns and most yards per catch in a career.

As he prepared for his first-ever game, the 1988 season opener against Michigan, Ismail's nerves worked on him. "I don't think I had caught one deep ball at receiver in three weeks," he said. It didn't seem to matter to head coach Lou Holtz. "I don't care if you catch it or not," he told the nervous freshman. "I'm going to put you out there and put the fear of God" in the Wolverines.

Ismail's nerves only got worse on game night. "I remember my legs feeling so weak that I didn't know if I could walk," he said about pre-game warm-ups. When Ismail entered the game, quarterback Tony Rice called for him to go deep. Rice then winked at the rookie to try to relax him; it didn't help.

Perhaps the fastest player in Irish history, Ismail blew past a

FIGHTING IRISH

Michigan back and was wide open. Rice's pass was on target. The ball "hit me in the hands and I dropped it," Ismail remembered.

The Irish had missed an easy touchdown. Ismail was deeply disappointed, but Holtz was unperturbed. On the sideline, he told the freshman, "Son, I told you I didn't care whether you caught the ball or not. You did exactly what I needed you to do."

He had indeed struck fear into the hearts of the UM backs.

We know disappointment. Friends betray us; we lose our jobs through no fault of our own; emotional distance grows between us and our children; the Irish lose; our dreams shatter.

Disappointment occurs when something or somebody fails to meet the expectations we have for them. Since people are people and can't do anything about that, they inevitably will disappoint us. What is absolutely crucial to our day-to-day living, therefore, is not avoiding disappointment but handling it.

One approach is to act as the old people of Israel did at the dedication of the temple. Instead of joyously celebrating the construction of a new place of worship, they wailed and moaned about the lost glories of the old one. They dwelled on the disappointment of the past rather than the wonders of the present reality.

Disappointment can paralyze us all, but only if we lose sight of an immutable truth: Our lives may not always be what we wish they were, but God is still good to us.

There's nothing disappointing about that.

Obviously, things got better from there.
— *Raghib Ismail on his disappointing start vs. Michigan*

Even in disappointing times, we can be confident that God is with us and therefore life is good.

THE SIMPLE LIFE

Read 1 John 1:5-10.

*"If we confess our sins, he is faithful and just and
will forgive us our sins and purify us from all
unrighteousness" (v. 9).*

With the 2001 national championship on the line, the Irish
women's basketball team relied on the simple formula they had
used all season: Get the ball to Ruth Riley.

Riley is a Notre Dame legend, the team's starting center from
1997-2001 and a two-time first-team All America. In 2001, she was
the Big East Player of the Year and the Associated Press National
Player of the Year. She also won the Naismith Award as the top
collegiate player in the country.

While making the Dean's List every semester, Riley finished
her career with school records for rebounds, blocked shots, and
field goal percentage. In 2000-01, the Irish won what was then a
school-record 34 games as they advanced to the championship
finals of the NCAA Tournament against Purdue.

With 1:01 to play, Riley hit a layup for two of her 28 points to
tie the game at 66. At the other end, she disrupted a Purdue layup attempt and grabbed her thirteenth rebound with 33 seconds
left. With 25.9 ticks to go, head coach Muffet McGraw called a timeout. Her plan was simple. "Everybody in the gym knew we were
going to Ruth," she said. Senior forward Kelley Siemon agreed.
"Regardless of the people around her, I was going to throw the

ball up," she said about getting the ball to Riley.

She did and Riley was fouled with 5.8 seconds left. Her Irish career ended in fairytale style when she hit both free throws for the 68-66 win and the national championship. "I can't think of a better way to go out," Riley said. Or, a simpler one.

Perhaps the simple life in America was doomed by the arrival of the programmable VCR, itself subsequently outmoded by more sophisticated technology. Since then, we've been on what seems to be an inevitably downward spiral into ever more complicated lives. Smartphones are smarter than their operators, and we all must know at least a little something about computers to survive.

But we might do well in our own lives to mimic the approach Muffet McGraw used to win a national title: Keep it simple. That is, we should approach our lives with the keen awareness that success requires simplicity, a sticking to the basics: Revere God, love our families, honor our country, do our best.

Theologians may make what God did in Jesus as complicated as quantum mechanics and the rules of dating in the 21st century, but God kept it simple for us: believe, trust, and obey. Believe in Jesus as the Son of God, trust that through him God makes possible our deliverance from our sins into Heaven, and obey God in the way he wants us to live.

That's the simple, true, and winning formula.

It's the same play we've been running all season. It's called 'Get the ball to Ruth.'
— *Muffet McGraw on the play vs. Purdue at game's end*

**God made it simple for us
when he showed up as Jesus.**

TOP SECRET

Read Romans 2:1-16.

"This will take place on the day when God will judge men's secrets through Jesus Christ, as my gospel declares" (v. 16).

John Huarte and Jack Snow had a secret.

Huarte is a Notre Dame legend, the senior quarterback who in 1964 won the Heisman Trophy before he even lettered. As the field general in what has been called "the miracle season that saved Notre Dame," he set twelve school passing records. A senior wide receiver who was an All-American that magical season, Snow was Huarte's favorite target. He set five school records including receptions, receiving yards, and touchdown catches in a season.

Over the summer of 1964, Snow and Huarte worked endlessly on pass routes in preparation for the season under first-year head coach Ara Parseghian. Gradually, a secret code emerged. Before the snap, Huarte would turn his head toward Snow and then turn the other way. If he glanced at Snow a second time, the code was in place: "The football is coming to you." They could get away with it because Huarte could tell within a few seconds after checking the defense whether Snow would be open.

At practice the week of the season opener, offensive backfield coach Tom Pagna told Huarte, "I'm on to you. I figured out your signal." He then revealed it. Before Huarte could reply, Pagna said, if the defense figures it out, "we're going to have to quash it.

Dig?" Then he added, "I don't think Ara's even figured it out yet. Let's see how long it takes."

An hour later, as Huarte walked back to the fieldhouse, Parseghian caught up with him and told him he was his starting quarterback for the opener. Then he added, "I know all about your little signal with Snow. I don't know if Pagna's even noticed it yet. But if the defense picks up on it, we'll have to cut it out."

Huarte just smiled and said, "You got it, Coach."

As John Huarte and Jack Snow were about their code, we have to be vigilant about the personal information we prefer to keep secret. Much information about us -- from credit reports to what movies we stream — is readily available to prying and persistent persons. In our information age, people we don't know may know a lot about us — or at least they can find out. And some of them may use this information for harm.

While diligence may allow us to be reasonably successful in keeping some secrets from the world at large, we should never deceive ourselves into believing we are keeping secrets from God. God knows everything about us, including the things we wouldn't want proclaimed at church. All our sins, shortcomings, mistakes, failures, quirks, prejudices, and desires — God knows all our would-be secrets.

But here's something God hasn't kept a secret: No matter what he knows about us, he loves us still.

There aren't any secrets in coaching.

— *Bobby Bowden*

**We have no secrets before God, and it's no secret
that he nevertheless loves us still.**

THE LAST WORD

Read Luke 9:22-27.

"The Son of Man . . . must be killed and on the third day be raised to life. . . . [S]ome who are standing here will . . . see the kingdom of God" (vv. 22, 27).

Before the game, the Seminoles did the talking and the jawing. When all was said and done, however, the Irish had the last word.

On Nov. 13, 1993, FSU and Notre Dame met in what was touted as the "Game of the Century." The Noles were undefeated and ranked No. 1; the Irish were undefeated and ranked No. 2. Both teams had 16-game win streaks. The game was so big that — for the first time ever — *ESPN College Gameday* left the home studios back in Connecticut and traveled to a game site.

As writer Austin Murphy put it, Florida State showed up at Notre Dame Stadium "with a decided lack of reverence." Before making the trip, a pair of Seminole players spoke of "Rock Knute," and another derided "the Three Horsemen." A Seminole wide receiver asked, "What's the Gipper?" Quarterback Charlie Ward told the world he wasn't going to South Bend for a history lesson.

Once the game started, though, the talking stopped. After the Noles scored on their first possession, wide receiver Adrian Jarrell used a crushing block from All-American tackle Aaron Taylor to cover 32 yards on a flanker reverse. The extra point tied the game, and then the Irish really silenced the Noles in the second quarter.

Junior tailback Lee Becton, who outrushed FSU by himself,

scored on a 26-yard burst off tackle. All-American safety Jeff Burris then scored from the 6 for a 21-7 halftime lead. Kevin Pendergrast's third-quarter field goal upped the count to 24-7.

The Noles pulled off a desperate rally until with three seconds left in the game, they sat at the Irish 14, trailing 31-24. Ward let loose with a pass into the end zone, and senior cornerback Shawn Wooden was there to make the play, batting the ball down.

The Irish thus had the last word, leaving the loquacious FSU players talking about the only thing they could: a rematch.

Why is it that, unlike the Irish against FSU, we often come up with the last word — the perfect zinger — only long after the incident that called for a smart and pithy rejoinder is over? "Man, I shoulda said that! That woulda fixed his wagon!" But it's too late.

Nobody in history, though, including us, could ever hope to match the man who had the greatest last word of them all: Jesus Christ. His enemies killed him and put him in a tomb, confident they were done with that nettlesome nuisance for good. Instead, they were unwitting participants in God's great plan of redemption, unintentionally giving the last word to Jesus. He has it still.

Jesus didn't go to that cross so he could die; he went to that cross so all those who follow him might live. Because of Jesus' own death on the cross, the final word for us is not our own death. Rather it is life, through our salvation in Jesus Christ.

We're hoping this was just Round 1.
— *FSU player talking after the defeat of 1993*

**With Jesus, the last word is always life
and never death.**

PLAN AHEAD

Read Psalm 33:1-15.

"The plans of the Lord stand firm forever, the purposes of his heart through all generations" (v. 11).

To help win a bowl game, Irish head coach Brian Kelly used an unusual strategy, one that many coaches would insist is doomed to failure: He used two quarterbacks.

As he prepared his team for the 2014 Music City Bowl and the favored LSU Tigers, Kelly figured he had to make the best use of the talent he had available to pull off the upset. He decided to ignore the conventional wisdom that declares a team performs best behind one quarterback rather than two.

So Kelly gave sophomore Malik Zaire his first start though Zaire's passing ability was an unknown. He had played in six games during the season and thrown only twenty passes.

The plan also meant getting plenty of playing time for senior Everett Golson, who had started every game during the regular season. Golson was a dual threat, a passer who had completed more than 60 percent of his throws during the season and had led the team with eight rushing touchdowns.

The plan worked out well. Zaire threw for 96 yards and ran for 96 more with a touchdown. Golson threw for 90 yards on 6-of-11 passing. The two-headed quarterback didn't commit a turnover.

Never was the plan more successful than on the game-winning drive. With the score tied at 28, the Irish got the ball at their own

7-yard line with 5:41 to play. They totally dominated the line of scrimmage, and LSU never got the ball back.

Notre Dame drove 71 yards in 14 plays. In succession, Zaire took three snaps, Golson three, Zaire two, Golson four, Zaire two. It was unlike anything Notre Dame had done all season. As time expired, senior Kyle Brindza booted a 32-yard field goal for the 31-28 win. Zaire was the holder.

In the excited Notre Dame locker room, receiver Chris Brown made his rounds, congratulating both quarterbacks.

Successful living takes planning. You go to school to improve your chances for a better paying job. You use blueprints to build your home. You plan for retirement. You map out your vacation to have the best time. You even plan your children — sometimes.

Your best-laid plans, however, sometime get wrecked by events and circumstances beyond your control. The economy goes into the tank; a debilitating illness strikes; a devastating storm hits. Since you aren't God, life seems capricious, and thus no plans — not even your most carefully contrived ones — are foolproof.

But you don't have to go it alone. God has plans for your life that guarantee success as God defines it if you will make him your planning partner. God's plan for your life includes joy, love, peace, kindness, gentleness, and faithfulness, all the elements necessary for truly successful living for today and for all eternity. And God's plan will not fail.

This was just utilizing both of their skills to get a win today.
— Brian Kelly on his two-quarterback strategy vs. LSU

Your plans may ensure a successful life;
God's plans will ensure a successful eternity.

DAY 11

A ROARING SUCCESS

Read Galatians 5:16-26.

"So I say, live by the Spirit. . . . The sinful nature desires what is contrary to the Spirit. . . . I warn you, as I did before, that those who live like this will not inherit the kingdom of God" (vv. 16, 17, 21).

The most successful sports program in Notre Dame history had its genesis in an automobile accident.

How's this for success? Eight national championships, an all-time winning percentage right at an unbelievable .900, and some three hundred All-Americas.

What sport is this? It's fencing, one of the oldest competitive teams in Irish athletic history.

The men's program began officially in 1936 as Notre Dame's eighth varsity sport. Since that beginning, the men do not have a losing record against a single one of their opponents. At one time they won 122 straight matches across a six-year stretch. They have also had streaks of 98, 90, and 80 wins.

The women's program was begun in 1976 and has been no less successful. They have had win streaks of 95 and 71 matches.

The squads competed separately for the national title until 1990 when the NCAA moved to a combined championship tournament. Only twice in that time have the Irish finished lower than fourth nationally; they have never finished worse than sixth.

So what does a car wreck have to do with all that success?

FIGHTING IRISH

Pedro DeLandero grew up in Mexico, graduated from Notre Dame in 1911, and returned to his homeland. Twenty years later, revolution drove him back to the university as a Spanish professor.

He was injured in a wreck in 1934. Doctors prescribed rehab through swimming, but DeLandero didn't like the water. He chose fencing instead and formed a small fencing club. That was the beginning of Notre Dame's most successful sports program.

Are you a successful person? Your answer, of course, depends upon how you define success. Is the measure of your success based on the number of digits in your bank balance, the square footage of your house, that title on your office door, the size of your boat?

Certainly the world determines success by wealth, fame, prestige, awards, and possessions. Our culture screams that life is all about gratifying your own needs and wants. If it feels good, do it. It's basically the Beach Boys' philosophy of life.

But all success of this type has one glaring shortcoming: You can't take it with you. Eventually, Daddy takes the T-bird away. Like life itself, all these things are fleeting.

A more lasting way to view success is through the lens of the spiritual rather than the physical. The goal becomes not money or backslaps by sycophants but eternal life spent with God. Success of that kind is forever.

The program's highlights span moments of high-pressure performances, displays of pure domination, and memorable upsets.
— 'Notre Dame Fencing Springs from Modest Beginnings'

**Success isn't permanent, and failure isn't fatal —
unless it's in your relationship with God.**

ONE TOUGH COOKIE

Read 2 Corinthians 11:21b-29.

"Besides everything else, I face daily the pressure of my concern for all the churches" (v. 28).

Anthony Johnson was so tough he once entered a boxing tournament so he could see what it was like to be hit in the face.

Johnson played fullback for Notre Dame from 1986-89. As the starter for the undefeated 1988 national champions, he was the team's fourth-leading rusher and its fifth-leading receiver. He won the Nick Petrosanti Award, presented to the player who exemplifies courage, loyalty, teamwork, and dedication.

Johnson was a quiet, laid-back man, the second oldest of nine children in a deeply Christian family. He took what was called "an unexpected delight" in the violence he discovered in football. He declared he "enjoyed being physical and not having to hold back." He said he liked hitting someone as much as he enjoyed being hit, admitting that the last part "may sound kind of off."

Johnson was a tough football player even in high school. During one of his games, he left the field for a few plays because of an injury. He went back in, expecting the pain to subside, but it didn't. After the game, his mother drove him to an emergency room to have him checked out. When he provided a urine sample, as Johnson put it, "I peed V8 juice, basically." He had played much of the game with a lacerated kidney.

While he was at Notre Dame, Johnson entered the school's

on-campus student boxing tournament, the Bengal Bouts. Why in the world would he do such a thing? "I'd never been hit in the face before and I wanted to see what it was like," he explained.

His playing style was as tough as he was, called by one writer "hard-fisted, punch-mouth football." The result was a player the offense could rely on. As quarterback Tony Rice observed, "If you needed two yards, he'll get it."

You don't have to be a tough Irish fullback as Anthony Johnson was to be tough. In America today, toughness isn't restricted to physical accomplishments and brute strength. Going to work every morning even when you feel bad, sticking by your rules for your children in a society that ridicules parental authority, making hard decisions about your aging parents' care often over their objections — you've got to be tough every day just to live honorably, decently, and justly.

Living faithfully requires toughness, too, though in America chances are you won't be imprisoned, stoned, or flogged this week for your faith as Paul was. Still, contemporary society exerts subtle, psychological, daily pressures on you to turn your back on your faith and your values. Popular culture promotes promiscuity, atheism, and gutter language; your children's schools have kicked God out; the corporate culture advocates amorality before the shrine of the almighty dollar.

You have to hang tough to keep the faith.

I'll tell ya, Anthony Johnson is tough.
> — ESPN *color commentator Kevin Kiley*

**Life demands more than mere physical toughness;
you must be spiritually tough too.**

FACING THE MUSIC

Read Psalm 98.

"Sing to the Lord a new song, for he has done marvelous things" (v. 1).

It didn't even get played at a Notre Dame athletic event until some ten years after its introduction, but today the "Notre Dame Victory March" has been officially recognized as the greatest of all fight songs.

The Rev. Michael Shea and his brother, John, both Notre Dame graduates, attended the Indiana and Michigan football games of 1908 together. What particularly struck them about the games was that both schools had a fight song and Notre Dame didn't.

The story goes that John brought up the idea of coming up with a song for the Irish. "I've got a tune running through my head," Michael responded. "I'll see you in a few days, and we'll go to work on it."

Conflicting stories survive, but Michael Shea later sat down at the piano in Sorin Hall and tinkered with the tune that was running around in his head. One account had the brothers working together in Sorin Hall with John coming up with the lyrics as they went along. They finished the composition the next day on the organ of Sacred Heart Church.

The "Notre Dame Victory March" made its public debut that winter when Michael played it on the organ of the Second Congregational Church in Holyoke. John Shea recalled that the first public performance of the song was on Easter Sunday, 1909, in the rotunda of the administration building. Surprisingly, it didn't become a fixture at athletic events until ten years later. According to the Notre Dame Guidebook, a member of the marching band nowadays will play the fight song about 4,000 times a year!

In 1969, what the Notre Dame faithful have always known was made official. As part of the centennial celebration of college football, the "Notre Dame Victory March" was declared to be the "greatest of all fight songs."

Maybe you can't play a lick or carry a tune in the proverbial bucket. Or perhaps you do know your way around a guitar or a keyboard and can sing the "Notre Dame Victory March" on karaoke night without closing the joint down.

Unless you're a professional musician, however, how well you play or sing really doesn't matter. What counts is that you have music in your heart and sometimes you have to turn it loose.

Worshipping God has always included music in some form. That same boisterous and musical enthusiasm you exhibit at the Irish games should be a part of the joy you have in your personal worship of God.

Take a moment to count the blessings in your life, all gifts from God. Then consider that God loves you, he always will, and he has arranged through Jesus for you to spend eternity with him. How can that song God put in your heart not burst forth?

I wonder if we couldn't work up a pep song [for] Notre Dame.
— *John Shea to his brother, Michael*

**You call it music; others may call it noise;
sent God's way, it's called praise.**

ALL OR NOTHING

Read Deuteronomy 6:4-9.

"Love the Lord your God with all your heart and with all your soul and with all your strength" (v. 5).

Quite simply, love for the Irish drives walk-on football players like Joe Recendez. In Recendez's case, however, that love drove him to do something extraordinary.

A sophomore at Notre Dame who had been a tight end in high school, Recendez felt the urge to play football again. He contacted coach Bob Chmiel, who told him simply to show up for winter workouts one day. He did in 1998.

Recendez recalled that there may have been tryouts, but he wasn't aware of them. "I was never told to go home," he said, laughing. No one ever told him formally that he was part of the team. He "just kept coming back and next thing you know the season started and I was on the team the rest of the time."

He kept coming back even after his position coach, Steve Addazio, told him that because of his size he probably wouldn't ever get on the field. "It's hard," Recendez admitted, "but I never once thought about quitting."

For Joe Recendez, though, life as a walk-on was harder than most; in fact, that he did it was a minor miracle. In May of 2000, before his senior year, Recendez was diagnosed with testicular cancer. He underwent surgery and radiation treatment. He took part in summer workouts despite the constant nausea the radiation effected. He subsisted mainly on crackers. "Sick as a dog, under medication, but he never complained — he never said anything," marveled offensive coordinator Kevin Rogers.

That fall Recendez received a scholarship. Then on Oct. 14, against Navy, he got in for four plays, 108 seconds. That was his complete Notre Dame career. Was it worth it, especially considering his battle with cancer? "Absolutely, "Recendez said.

For him, it was simple. He loved Notre Dame that much.

Unlike Joe Recendez, who gave Notre Dame his all, too many sports fans cheer loudly when their team is winning championships, but they're the first to criticize or turn silent when losses and disappointments come. They're fair-weather fans.

The true fans stick with the Irish no matter what, which is exactly the way God commands us to love him. Sure, this mandate is eons old, but the principle it established in our relationship with God has not changed. If anything, it has gained even more immediacy in our materialistic, secular culture that demands we love and worship anything and anybody but God.

Moreover, since God gave the original command, he has sent us Jesus. Thus, we today are even more indebted to God's grace and have even more reason to love God than did the Israelites to whom the original command was given.

God gave us everything; in return, we are to love him with everything we have and everything we are.

For the walk-ons, every single one of us loves Notre Dame.
— *Joe Recendez*

**With all we have and all we are
— that's the way we are to love God.**

AT A LOSS

Read Philippians 3:1-9.

"I consider everything a loss compared to the surpassing greatness of knowing Christ Jesus my Lord, for whose sake I have lost all things" (v. 8).

A day of triumph for Mike Brey was also a day of loss.

In 2000, Brey took charge of the Notre Dame's men's basketball program, which had gone a decade without landing in the NCAA Tournament. Through 2016, the Irish have appeared in eleven of the last sixteen playoffs. In 2014-15, they finished 32-6, won the ACC Tournament in their second year in the conference, and came within a shot of upsetting Kentucky to reach the Final Four.

Before his team's game against Butler in the third round of the 2015 NCAA Tournament, Brey told his players somebody had asked him why he had been smiling all day. "Because I have a great team, baby," he said. "I've got a great team." After the game, a 67-64 overtime win that sent the Irish to the Sweet Sixteen, Brey burst into his locker room and shouted, "Is it past midnight?" A player shouted back that it was. "Well, it's my birthday," Brey said. Then he thanked his team for a great birthday present.

Only then did the players learn that the day had truly been a long, difficult one for their coach. The morning of the game, Brey's mother had died. "It shows how he feels about his kids," said athletic director Jack Swarbrick. "That's so preeminent with him, not wanting to be a distraction or not being available."

Brey said he never thought about skipping the game after his brother encouraged him to stay with the team and "Beat Butler." The Irish coach was also confident his mother would have wanted him to stay with his team. A swimmer at Purdue, she competed in the 1956 Olympics. Swarbrick agreed that Brey's parents would have wanted their son to be with his players. "That was their lives. They were coaches. They were teachers," he said.

Still, a day of great triumph was a day of great loss for Brey.

Maybe, as it was with Mike Brey, it was when a family member died. Perhaps it wasn't so staggeringly tragic: your family pet died, your best friend moved away, or a sibling left home. Sometime in your youth or early adult life, though, you learned that loss is a part of life.

Loss inevitably diminishes your life, but loss and the grief that accompanies it are part of the price of loving. When you first encountered loss, you learned that you were virtually helpless to prevent it or escape it.

There is life after loss, though, because you have one sure place to turn. Jesus can share your pain and ease your suffering; but he doesn't stop there. Through the loss of his own life, he has transformed death — the ultimate loss — into the ultimate gain of eternal life. In Jesus lies the promise that one day loss itself will die.

Probably the real driving force behind everything I've done.
— *Mike Brey on his mother*

Jesus not only eases the pain of our losses
but transforms the loss caused by death
into the gain of eternal life.

THE SUB

Read Galatians 3:10-14.

"Christ redeemed us from the curse of the law by becoming a curse for us" (v. 13).

The Irish were in a fight for their lives when starting quarterback Malik Zaire went down with a broken ankle. That left the team in the hands of an untested sub — which was quite all right.

According to junior wide receiver Will Fuller, Zaire, a junior making only his second start, "played a dang near perfect game for us" in the 2015 season opener. Zaire completed 19 of 22 passes for 313 yards to lead Notre Dame to a 38-3 rout of Texas. Only Steve Beuerlein's 10-of-11 passing against Colorado in 1984 was a more accurate performance than Zaire's game against Texas.

The following Saturday, the fired-up Virginia Cavaliers gave the ninth-ranked Irish all they wanted in a bid for a big upset. The game took what seemed to be a disastrous turn for Notre Dame when Zaire's game and season ended with his injury with 1:15 left in the third quarter. At the time, the Irish led only 19-14.

Backup quarterback DeShone Kizer trotted onto the field for "his first meaningful collegiate playing time." On his first play, he handed off to senior running back C.J. Prosise, who skirted the right side for a 24-yard touchdown run and a 26-14 Irish lead.

After that, though, the Virginia offense went on a tear and took a 27-26 lead with a touchdown with 1:54 left in the game. The Irish and their substitute quarterback then had 80 yards to cover and

108 seconds to do it in. No problem.

The first crucial play came on fourth-and-two at the 28; Kizer got four on a keeper. Then, with 12 seconds left, Kizer etched his name into Notre Dame lore when he lofted a 39-yard touchdown pass to Fuller. He then ended his day with a pass to Torii Hunter, Jr., for the two-point conversion and a 34-27 Irish win.

The sub finished with 8-of-12 passing and two touchdowns.

Wouldn't it be cool if you had a substitute like DeShone Kizer for all of life's hard stuff? Telling of a death in the family? Call in your sub. Breaking up with the person you've been seeing? Job interview? Crucial presentation at work? Let the sub handle it.

We do have such a substitute, but not for the matters of life. Instead, Jesus is our substitute for matters of life and death. Since Jesus has already made it, we don't have to make the sacrifice God demands for forgiveness and salvation.

One of the most pathetic aspects of our contemporary times is that many people deny Jesus Christ and then desperately cast about for a substitute for him. Mysticism, human philosophies such as Scientology, false religions such as Hinduism and Islam, cults, New Age approaches that preach self-fulfillment without responsibility or accountability — they and others like them are all pitiful, inadequate substitutes for Jesus.

There is no substitute for Jesus. It's Jesus or nothing.

Kizer became a folk hero, the kind of real-life scene stealer[s] that sometimes encore their way forever into Notre Dame lore.
— Writer Eric Hansen on DeShone Kizer vs. Virginia

There is no substitute for Jesus,
the consummate substitute.

THE FAME GAME

Read 1 Kings 10:1-10, 18-29.

"King Solomon was greater in riches and wisdom than all the other kings of the earth. The whole world sought audience with Solomon" (vv. 23-24).

John Lattner was duly famous for winning the 1953 Heisman Trophy. He also garnered considerable fame for spending time with Marilyn Monroe.

Prior to his senior season (1953), a major change in the rules helped make Lattner so famous that he appeared on the cover of *Time*. After twelve seasons of allowing unlimited substitutions, the NCAA decreed that players had to play both ways. In effect, that change turned Lattner loose. He played halfback and defensive back, punted, and returned kicks. He set the school record for career all-purpose yards, broken by Vagas Ferguson (1976-79). Not only did he win the Heisman, but he twice won the Maxwell Award as the nation's top player.

As a sophomore in 1951, Lattner had achieved an envious bit of fame when the Irish played Southern Cal in Los Angeles. He and some other players learned Monroe was making a movie at a local studio, so they decided to drop by unannounced. As Lattner put it, kicker Bobby Joseph "could talk like a million dollars." Thanks to Joseph's sweet tongue, they got into the studio.

Not only that, but the guys spent an hour or so visiting with Monroe in her dressing room. When she brought out some publicity photos, Lattner told her to sign his, "Dear John, Thank you for the wonderful night we had together. Love and kisses, Marilyn." She did it and then added her phone number.

Monroe even drove the players back to their hotel. "There were five of us in that little car, but we had a ball," Lattner said.

Have you ever wanted to be famous like John Lattner or Marilyn Monroe? Hanging out with other rich and famous people, having folks with microphones listen to what you say, throwing money around like toilet paper, meeting adoring and clamoring fans, signing autographs, and posing for the paparazzi before you climb into your imported sports car?

Many of us yearn to be famous, well-known in the places and by the people that we believe matter. That's all fame amounts to: strangers knowing your name and your face.

The truth is that you are already famous where it really does matter, which excludes TV's talking heads, screaming teenagers, rapt moviegoers, or D.C. power brokers. You are famous because Almighty God knows your name, your face, and everything else there is to know about you.

If a persistent photographer snapped you pondering this fame — the only kind that has eternal significance — would the picture show the world unbridled joy or the shell-shocked expression of a mug shot?

She was so delightful. What a gal!
— *John Lattner on Marilyn Monroe*

You're already famous because God knows your name and your face, which may be either reassuring or terrifying.

DAY 18

UNEXPECTEDLY

Read Matthew 24:36-51.

*"No one knows about that day or hour, not even the
angels in heaven, nor the Son, but only the Father" (v. 36).*

The Irish have had some wildly successful football seasons that
came as no surprise. What the team did in 1973, however, was
totally unexpected.

The 1972 season ended with a big, loud thud with back-to-
back thrashings from Southern Cal and Nebraska (in the Orange
Bowl). The final record was 8-3, and Notre Dame Head coach Ara
Paraseghian called the losses "three of the most stunning defeats
in Notre Dame history."

Optimism generally was tempered heading into 1973 largely
because of the finish in '72 and the number of young players the
Irish would play. But Parseghian turned his legendary intensity
loose on his coaches, his players, and himself to challenge them.

He also made some adjustments, the biggest of which was
changing the team's defensive alignment. He threw every starting
job up for grabs. (Four starters from '72 were relegated to backup
roles.) He also instituted some new rules for his team (such as
hair length) to instill discipline and cohesion.

In addition to the new formations, the new players, and the
new rules, the team got a boost from two unexpected factors:
some critical team chemistry and contributions from freshmen
Ross Browner, Luther Bradley, Willie Fry, and Al Hunter.

FIGHTING IRISH

The result was a 5-0 start, but the wins were against teams that would finish with losing records. The first real test came on Oct. 27 against sixth-ranked Southern Cal. The underdog youngsters beat the Trojans 23-14. Junior halfback Eric Penick broke USC's back with an 85-yard touchdown run in the third quarter.

Notre Dame would not be tested again until the Sugar Bowl, a 24-13 upset of top-ranked Alabama. Unexpectedly, the Irish were 11-0 and were college football's national champions.

Just like the pundits who underrated the 1973 Irish, we think we've got everything figured out and under control, and then something unexpected happens. About the only thing we can expect from life with any certainty is the unexpected.

God is that way too, suddenly showing up to remind us he's still around. A friend who calls and tells you he's praying for you, a hug from your child or grandchild, a lone lily that blooms in your yard — unexpected moments when the divine comes crashing into our lives with such clarity that it takes our breath away and brings tears to our eyes.

But why shouldn't God do the unexpected? The only factor limiting what God can do in our lives is the paucity of our own faith. We should expect the unexpected from God, this same deity who caught everyone by surprise by unexpectedly coming to live among us as a man, and who will return when we least expect it.

It was unexpected. I thought we were a year away.
— Ara Parseghian on the 1973 season

God continually does the unexpected,
like showing up as Jesus,
who will return unexpectedly.

BEING DIFFERENT

Read Daniel 3.

*"We want you to know, O king, that we will not serve
your gods or worship the image of gold you have set up"*
(v. 18).

At Notre Dame, Vanessa Pruzinsky was just different.

First of all, Pruzinsky was different because of her athletic abi-lity. She was a defender on the Irish women's soccer team from 1999-2003, starting 94 of the 96 matches she played in. She was the Big East Rookie of the Year in 1999 and first-team All-Big East in 2001. She finished up by being named the 2003-04 Big East Female Scholar-Athlete of the Year. She graduated "as one of the best to ever play under coach Randy Waldrum."

Secondly, Pruzinsky was different because she wasn't just bril-liant on the field, she was brilliant in the classroom. In the spring of 2003, she became the first chemical engineering major in 29 years and the first female ever to graduate from Notre Dame with a 4.0 grade-point-average. She admitted to often studying more than seven hours a day. With headphones on and textbook open, she relied on one CD of acoustic guitar music the whole time to provide ambient noise. "If the music had words," she said, "I'd get distracted."

Thirdly, Pruzinsky was different because — well, she was dif-ferent. She was, in fact, notoriously absent-minded. "For someone so smart, you'd never know it sometimes by talking to her," said

Waldrum. Pruzinsky's teammates often told stories about her, like the fact that even after she had lived on campus for five years, she still used printouts of Yahoo! Maps to get most places. They said her locker was in such disarray that she never could find her training gear. Finally, the team gave her two more lockers to help her out.

Vanessa Pruzinzky was different, and she made her mark at Notre Dame as few ever have or ever will.

While we live in a secular society that constantly pressures us to conform to its principles and values, we serve a risen Christ who calls us to be different. Therein lies the great conflict of the Christian life in contemporary America.

But how many of us really consider that even in our secular society we struggle to conform? We are all geeks in a sense. We can never truly conform because we were not created by God to live in such a sin-filled world in the first place. Thus, when Christ calls us to be different by following and espousing Christian beliefs, principles, and practices, he is summoning us to the lifestyle we were born for.

The most important step in being different for Jesus is realizing and admitting who we really are: We are children of God; we are Christians. Only secondarily are we citizens of a secular world. That world both scorns and disdains us for being different; Jesus both praises and loves us for it.

She can be a little ding-y.
— *Soccer head coach Randy Waldrum on Vanessa Pruzinsky*

The lifestyle Jesus calls us to is different from that of the world, but it is the way we were born to live.

AGAINST ALL ODDS

Read John 16:19-33.

"In this world you will have trouble. But take heart! I have overcome the world" (v. 33b).

Kyle Brindza had to overcome the odds just to walk and run, let alone become an athlete and a collegiate kicker.

While the other children played football with their buddies or kicked a soccer ball around, Brindza was in the hospital undergoing another surgery. He was born with clubfoot. His right foot was twisted inward so badly that he underwent multiple surgeries before he was in the sixth grade. There were so many of them that he lost count.

"I was worried about Kyle just being able to walk," his mother said. She had good reason. Her son essentially had no heel on his right foot as the side of the foot was attached directly to the bottom of his calf. The tendons had to be cut and repositioned. The surgeries left his ankle and foot covered with what looked like battle scars.

For Brindza, normal life was hard casts, walking boots, corrective shoes, corrective bars, and hospital stays. "I thought a cast was just normal," he said. "I pretty much learned how to walk and crawl in a cast, let alone run."

The final procedure came when Brindza was in the sixth grade. He had surgery around Thanksgiving and was playing soccer by Christmas. His foot improved and so did his athleticism. In high school, his kicking skills drew attention from major colleges.

While he was coaching at Cincinnati, Brian Kelly recruited Brindza but couldn't come up with an offer good enough to lure him. That changed when Kelly moved to Notre Dame.

From 2011-14, Brindza set the school record with 57 career field goals. His 25 field goals in 2012 is the season record; his five field goals is the record for a game.

We each have a choice to make about how we live. We can merely survive or we can overcome as Kyle Brindza did.

We often hear inspiring stories of people who triumph by overcoming especially daunting obstacles. Those barriers may be physical or mental disabilities or great personal tragedies or injustice. When we hear of them, we may well respond with a little prayer of thanksgiving that life has been kinder to us.

But all people of faith, no matter how drastic the obstacles they face, must ultimately overcome the same opponent: the Satan-infested world. Some do have it tougher than others, but we all must fight daily to remain confident and optimistic.

Mere survival with little or no hope results when we surrender our trust in God's involvement in our daily lives. To overcome, however, is to stand up to the world and fight its temptations that would erode the armor of our faith in Jesus Christ.

Today is a day for you to overcome by remaining faithful. The very hosts of Heaven wait to hail the conquering hero.

It's kind of nice to have the odds against you and prove everyone wrong.
— Kyle Brindza

Life's difficulties provide us a chance
to experience the true joy of victory in Jesus.

LAUGH IT UP

Read Genesis 21:1-7.

"Sarah said, 'God has brought me laughter, and everyone who hears about this will laugh with me'" (v. 6).

Zygmont "Ziggy" Czarobski's philosophy may well have been to leave 'em crying on the football field and laughing off it.

Czarobski played tackle on the national championship teams of 1943, 1946, and 1947. After serving in the military in 1944 and '45, he turned down what he called "an unheard of figure for a pro tackle" to return to Notre Dame. He was first-team All-America as a senior in 1947 and was inducted into the College Football Hall of Fame in 1977.

Czarobski was a larger than life character, perhaps as famous for the way he lived and laughed off the field as he was for his exploits on it. For instance, on the questionnaire he filled out as an incoming student for the school's publicity office, he listed his church preference as "red brick." Among his hobbies was "surf-riding"; Czarobski was from the South Side of Chicago. When he showed up for school in 1942, he brought a load of Polish sausage and cheese. "I don't know if they'll feed me right," he said, "and I'm not taking any chances."

A dismayed head coach Frank Leahy discovered Ziggy taking a shower before practice one day. His explanation? "Coach, it just gets too crowded afterward." Ziggy listened politely in a New York elevator one day while General Omar Bradley complimented

FIGHTING IRISH

the Irish team. His reply? "Thanks, General. And speaking for the rest of the team, we sure have enjoyed your battles."

Ziggy wasn't much help at practice the day Leahy decided his team needed to return to the fundamentals. The coach began his earnest presentation with "Gentlemen, this is a football." Ziggy interrupted to say, "Hold it, Coach. Not so fast."

Quarterback John Lujack said Ziggy "used to tell people he was in school for two terms — Roosevelt's and Truman's."

As Zygmont Czarobski did, stand-up comedians find humor in the world. That's the basis for their success because it's often hard for us to do that. "Laughter is foolish," an acerbic Solomon wrote in Ecclesiastes 2:2, his angst overwhelming him because he couldn't find much if anything in his world to laugh at.

We know how he felt. When we take a good look around at this world we live in, can we really find much to laugh at? It seems everywhere we look we find not just godlessness but ongoing and pervasive tragedy and misery.

Well, we can recognize as Sarah did that in God's innumerable gifts lie irresistible laughter. The great gift of Jesus provides us with more than enough reason to laugh no matter our situation. Through God's grace in Jesus Christ, we can laugh at death, at Satan, at the very gates of hell, at the world's pain.

Because they are of this world, our tears will pass. Because it is of God, our laughter will remain — forever.

Everybody has a Ziggy story.
— All-American tackle Bill Fischer, a teammate of Ziggy Czarobski's

Of the world, sorrow is temporary;
of God, laughter is forever.

DAY 22

MEMORY LOSS

Read 1 Corinthians 11:17-29.

"[D]o this in remembrance of me" (v. 24).

The Notre Dame faithful remembered what Pat Terrell did. In 1999, his last-minute play against Miami was named the most memorable moment in Irish football history.

Emotion ran so high for the Miami game of Oct. 15, 1988, that officials agreed to end the annual game in 1990 in "the interest of the schools, the students, and collegiate sports." 1988 was the year of the famous — or infamous — "Catholics vs. Convicts" T-shirts. A student magazine printed a poster of Miami head coach Jimmy Johnson that declared, "Avoid the Rush, Hate Miami Early. Only 198 Days Left!"

The game didn't appear to be one in which the fourth-ranked Irish could gain some revenge for four straight defeats at the hands of the Canes. The defending national champions, Miami was ranked No. 1 and had won thirty-six regular season games in a row, including twenty straight road games.

Nevertheless, what took place was "one of the most hard-fought, back-and-forth games in Notre Dame history." The Irish led most of the day, but as the clock wound down, the Hurricanes rushed downfield to save themselves. With 45 seconds left to play, they scored on fourth down to cut Notre Dame's lead to 31-30. They then went for the win with the two-point conversion.

Terrell made just his second start at free safety that day and would go on to be an All-American in 1989. He was lined up opposite a receiver he had played against in high school. "We just grinned," Terrell said, "and I had a feeling then that they might be looking to throw the ball his way."

They were. The pass soared, and Terrell and the receiver went up as one. "With just the very tips of his fingers," Terrell batted the ball away, making a never-to-be forgotten play.

Memory makes us who we are. Whether our memories appear as pleasant reverie or unnerving nightmares, they shape us and to a large extent determine both our actions and our reactions. Alzheimer's is so terrifying because it steals our memory from us, and in the process we lose ourselves. We disappear.

The greatest tragedy of our lives is that God remembers. In response to that photographic memory, he condemns us for our sin. Paradoxically, the greatest joy of our lives is that God remembers. In response to that memory, he came as Jesus to wash even the memory of our sins away.

God uses memory as a tool through which we encounter revival. At the Last Supper, Jesus instructed his disciples and us to remember. In sharing this unique meal with fellow believers and remembering Jesus and his actions, we meet Christ again, not just as a memory, but as an actual living presence. To remember is to keep our faith alive.

Irish fans young and old provide countless memories [of where they were] when Notre Dame beat Miami in 1988.

— *Writer Joe Garner*

**Because we remember Jesus,
God will not remember our sins.**

DAY 23

AS A RULE

Read Luke 5:27-32.

"Why do you eat and drink with tax collectors and 'sinners'?" (v. 30b)

Nick Ossello and his dad used an NCAA rule to resurrect a childhood dream he had given up on.

Ossello grew up intent on being a college football player, and he was a star quarterback in high school. He had a problem, however; he was an even better lacrosse player. When some of the nation's top programs came forward with scholarship offers, he couldn't turn them down. He chose Notre Dame.

"A fearless midfielder," Ossello played as a freshman in 2012 and soon "carve[d] out a fierce reputation on the lacrosse field as a relentless force." He started both his junior and senior seasons and played a major role in cementing Notre Dame lacrosse as a powerhouse. The team earned berths in the NCAA Tournament each of Ossello's four seasons with the 2014 squad advancing to the finals. In his last game, he scored a goal with nine seconds left in regulation to force overtime in the 2015 NCAA semifinals.

But the Irish eventually lost that game, and Ossello's career as a college athlete was over, his dream of playing college football unfulfilled. Or so it seemed.

Somehow, in a conversation between Nick and his dad, the two discovered the NCAA rule that allows a fifth year of eligibility in a different sport. Ossello subsequently reached out to

FIGHTING IRISH

some former coaches and was all set to transfer to Montana for a single season of football. That all changed when the Irish coaches learned of his intentions. They were familiar with his lacrosse career, and they offered him the chance to walk on.

Ossello did and — thanks to a rule — realized his childhood dream. Listed on the roster as a safety, he played in six games on special teams for the Irish in 2015.

You live by rules that others set up. Some lender determined the interest rate on your mortgage and your car loan. You work hours and shifts somebody else established. Someone else decided what day your garbage gets picked up and what school district your house is in.

Jesus encountered societal rules also. These included a strict set of religious edicts that dictated what company he should keep, what people, in other words, were fit for him to socialize with, talk to, or share a meal with. Jesus simply ignored the rules. He chose love instead of mindless obedience, and he demonstrated his disdain for society's rules by mingling with the outcasts, the lowlifes, the poor, and the misfits.

You, too, have to choose when you find yourself in the presence of someone whom society or your peers deem to be undesirable. Will you choose the rules or will you choose love?

Are you willing to be a rebel for love — as Jesus was for you?

[Dad and I] thought that was kind of neat.
— Nick Ossello on the rule that allowed him to play football in 2015

Society's rules dictate who is acceptable and who is not, but love in the name of Jesus knows no such distinctions.

GRACIOUS HOSTS

Read 2 Kings 4:8-17.

"Let's make a small room on the roof and put in it a bed and a table, a chair and a lamp for him. Then he can stay there whenever he comes to us" (v. 10).

Irish lore has it that a conversation between wives about hospitality played a key part in the establishment of one of college football's greatest rivalries.

The annual Notre Dame-Southern Cal get-together "is considered one of the most important in college football and is often called the greatest intersectional rivalry" of them all. With the exception of three seasons during World War II, the two institutions have played every year since 1926.

More than one story survives about how "the oldest and most prestigious intersectional rivalry in the country" got its start. The classic explanation, though, has become known as the "conversation-between-wives" story.

In 1925, Gwynn Wilson, USC's graduate manager of athletics, and his bride of six months took a train trip to talk to Knute Rockne about a home-and-home series. Busy with preparations for the Nebraska game, Rockne said he'd buy a ticket to Chicago for Gwynn and his wife and they could talk on the train.

When the two did get together, Rockne balked. He said his team was already traveling too much; it had even picked up the nickname of Ramblers, which he didn't like. He was also trying to set up more games with Big Ten schools. Wilson figured the idea was dead in the water.

Not so. While the two men were reaching an impasse, their wives were having a friendly conversation of their own. Marion Wilson told Bonnie Rockne "how nice Southern California was and how hospitable the people were." That won her over. When Rockne returned to the compartment, she talked him into setting up the game. He met with Wilson again and the series was on.

Hospitality just seems to be part of the American psyche. You open your home to the neighborhood kids, to your friends, to the stranger whose car broke down in the rain, to the stray cat that showed up hungry and hollering. You invite friends over often, even that misguided fellow who isn't a Notre Dame fan. You let family members overstay their welcome without grumbling.

Hospitality was an essential element of the cultures of Biblical times also. Travelers braved innumerable dangers: everything from lions to bandits to deadly desert heat. Finding a temporary haven thus often became quite literally a matter of life and death.

Since hospitality has through the ages been a sign of a loving and generous nature, it is not surprising that almighty God himself is a gracious host. He welcomes you, not as a stranger, but as an adopted child. One glorious day this hospitable God will open the doors of his place for you — and never ask you to leave.

If it hadn't been for Mrs. Wilson talking to Mrs. Rockne, there wouldn't have been a [Notre Dame-Southen Cal] series.
— *USC athletics manager Gwynn Wilson*

Hospitality is an outward sign of the inward loving, generous, and godly nature of the host.

DAY 25

NO APOLOGIES

Read Acts 4:1-21.

"For we cannot help speaking about what we have seen and heard" (v. 20).

Notre Dame head coach Elmer Layden once flew into a rage after a game and wound up apologizing all over the place.

Along with halfbacks Don Miller and Jim Crowley and quarterback Harry Stuhldreher, Layden, a fullback, was one of the Four Horsemen immortalized by legendary sportswriter Grantland Rice after Notre Dame's 13-7 win over Army in 1924. He returned to South Bend in 1934 and coached the Irish for seven seasons, compiling a record of 47-13-3.

Layden's 1940 squad finished the season on the road against Southern Cal and won the game 10-6. When it ended, Layden was still furious over what he regarded as a horrendous pass interference call on sophomore back Bernie Crimmins at a crucial time late in the game. Described as "usually the model of post-game decorum," the head coach rushed onto the field after the final gun and cornered the offending official.

Layden told the hapless ref what he thought of him and then "snarled the same complaints" at the Southern Cal head coach and the school's athletic director. Not yet satisfied, Layden next lit into USC's chancellor, asserting he was "sick and tired of the job turned in by West Coast officials every time that Notre Dame played there."

His anger subsiding and his tirade over, Layden made his way into the dressing room and was immediately approached by Crimmins. "Coach, I'm sorry," the player said, "but I pushed the Trojan receiver."

A mortified Layden rushed out of the door, spotted the USC chancellor, and apologized. Then he sought out the Southern Cal coach and AD and even the referee "to murmur his apologies."

As Elmer Layden did, we usually apologize when we wrong or injure another person whether it's bumping into someone in the supermarket, causing an automobile accident, or being uncharacteristically harsh or cruel. Courtesy, forthrightness, our sense of justice, and our Christ-centered desire to repair the damage to a relationship demand apologies from us sometime.

But too many Christians in the increasingly hostile environment that is contemporary America find themselves apologizing for their faith and the temerity they display in inviting someone to church or saying the name of Jesus in their presence. We shouldn't. To apologize for our faith is to declare, in effect, that we are ashamed of Jesus.

Like Peter and John, we do not have to tell anyone we're sorry for our faith or abashedly try to excuse our actions in the name of Christ. We are Christians, heart and soul. And don't those who purposely flaunt their behavior in Christians' faces tell us, "If you don't like it, live with it"? We're just doing the same. Only in our case, we're talking about living eternally.

That dang Crimmins!
   — *Elmer Layden recalling his anger and his apologies vs. USC*

We should never apologize for Jesus.

HEART OF THE MATTER

Read Matthew 6:19-24.

"Store up for yourselves treasures in heaven . . . . For where your treasure is, there your heart will be also" (vv. 20, 21).

Carlyle Holiday's dilemma was simple, if difficult. His head told him to leave Notre Dame; his heart told him to stay.

Holiday arrived in South Bend in 2000 as "a breathtaking 6-foot-3, 215-pound athlete" who had never played anything but quarterback on offense and had never wanted to. From 2000-02, he played in 31 games, starting 21 of them.

The highlight of Holiday's time at Notre Dame was his junior season. He started twelve games, leading the Irish to nine wins. Overall, the team finished 10-3 and ranked 17th in the country.

But Holiday and the team started slowly in 2003. In the first three games, he threw four interceptions and only one touchdown pass as the Irish went 1-2. Head coach Tyrone Willingham pulled his senior in favor of freshman Brady Quinn, who would set a number of school records, including most completions (929) and most touchdown passes (95). As a senior in 2006, Quinn won the Johnny Unitas Golden Arm Award as the nation's best college quarterback and the Maxwell Award as the country's best college player. He was a second-team All-America.

Meanwhile, Holiday faced a tough choice: He could adapt to a new position or he could leave Notre Dame. "I had been playing quarterback since I was seven," he recalled. "To have that taken away was tough." So Holiday's head told him to pack his bags, transfer, and play quarterback somewhere else.

His heart said something else. "I had so many great relationships and I had so much respect for the program," he said. "As you're there and you're playing football, you realize how special [it] is." If it had been any other school, he would have left, he said.

His heart and his love for Notre Dame overruled his head. He stayed and switched to wide receiver and returned punts. He caught five passes and went on to play four seasons in the NFL.

As with Carlyle Holiday, we often face decisions in life that force us to choose between our heart and our head. Our head says take that job with the salary increase; our heart says don't relocate because the kids are doing so well. Our head declares now is not the time to start a relationship; our heart insists that we're in love.

We wrestle with our head and our heart as we determine what matters the most to us. When it comes to the ultimate priority in our lives, though, our head and our heart tell us it's Jesus.

What that means for our lives is a resolution of the conflict we face daily: that of choosing between the values of our culture and a life of trust in and obedience to God. The two may occasionally be compatible, but when they're not, our head tells us what Jesus wants us to do; our heart tells us how right it is that we do it.

If it's something that you really want to do in your heart, stick with it and work hard and just keep your faith in Christ.
— Former all-pro defensive back Ty Law

In our struggle with competing value systems, our head and our heart lead us to follow Jesus.

HAVE COURAGE

Read 1 Corinthians 16:13-14.

"Be on your guard; stand firm in the faith; be men of courage; be strong" (v. 13).

Head coach Digger Phelps called David Rivers "the best player I had over my Notre Dame career." He may also have been the most courageous.

A point guard, Rivers was a third-team All-American in 1986-87 and a second team selection as a senior in 1987-88. He lettered all four seasons, and his name is still all over the Irish record book. He was a cocaptain as a senior.

On March 29, 1987, the U.S. Basketball Writers honored Rivers as the nation's Most Courageous Athlete of 1987. The award stemmed from an accident on Aug. 24, 1986, in which Rivers was thrown through the windshield of the vehicle he was riding in. During his violent exit, Rivers' stomach was virtually sliced in two, a 15-inch gash, by the broken glass.

Despite a severe injury of his own, the driver, a former Irish basketball player, sprinted to a nearby house and got help. He returned to the scene and used his shirt to cover Rivers' wound. He also talked to him and prayed with him until the paramedics arrived. Phelps later told the distraught former player that he had saved Rivers' life. Rivers underwent several hours of surgery just to clean the debris out of his stomach.

Incredibly and courageously, he was back in class by Sept. 15

and played 34 minutes in the season opener on Nov. 16. Phelps said Rivers carried the team to the Sweet 16 when he scored 74 points in the first three NCAA games.

Had the Irish made it to the Final Four, they wouldn't have had Rivers. The week of the Final Four, he had emergency surgery because bands of scar tissue were twisting his bowels.

When we speak of courage, we often think of heroic actions such as that displayed by soldiers during wartime or firefighters during an inferno. But as David Rivers' recovery from his awful accident demonstrates, there is another aspect to courage.

What made Rivers' daily life courageous and admirable after his injury was not the absence of fear, which often results from foolhardiness or a dearth of relevant information. Rather, Rivers' courage showed itself in his determined refusal to let fear debilitate him and keep him from playing basketball again.

This is the courage God calls upon us to demonstrate in our faith lives. When Paul urged the Christians in Corinth to "be men of courage," he wasn't telling them to rush into burning buildings. He was admonishing them to be strong and sure in their faith.

This courageous attitude is an absolute necessity for American Christians today when our faith is under attack as never before. Our spiritual courage reveals itself in our proclaiming the name of Jesus no matter what forces are arrayed against us.

Fittingly, David Rivers accepted the Most Courageous Athlete of 1987 award from his hospital room over the phone.

— Digger Phelps

To be courageous for Jesus is to speak his name boldly no matter what Satan uses against us.

DAY 28

BE PREPARED

Read Matthew 10:5-23.

*"I am sending you out like sheep among wolves. Therefore
be as shrewd as snakes and as innocent as doves" (v. 16).*

Frank Leahy always had his team prepared — even when that
preparation included pith helmets.

Leahy coached at Notre Dame for eleven seasons (1941-43, '46-
53). His record was 87-11-9 with six undefeated seasons, four national championships, and one stretch of 39 games without a loss.
He was inducted into the College Football Hall of Fame in 1970.
A combination of health problems and the administration's decision to de-emphasize football forced Leahy to step down at Notre
Dame when he was only 45.

Leahy believed that games were won on the practice field with
careful and exacting preparation. It was said of Leahy that his
teams never had a practice without hitting and that his quarterbacks often caught snaps until their hands bled.

Perhaps no single game demonstrates the lengths Leahy would
go to to prepare his team than the Texas game of 1952. Prior to
the game, Leahy astounded everyone by ordering 36 pith helmets.
"Nobody knew what he wanted them for," assistant coach Joe
McArdle said. Leahy then said he wanted the Notre Dame bench
on the same side of the field as that of the Longhorns. A dismayed
McArdle pulled a bluff, telling the stadium field crew the Texas
head coach had okayed the move.

FIGHTING IRISH

In the fourth quarter, the Irish sat in the shade with the Long-horns. Moreover, the pith helmets had kept the sun off the players earlier in the day. Leahy had also brought extra ice to put in the helmets. "The players had air conditioning," McArdle said.

All the preparation paid off when the Irish players "had a lot left in the fourth quarter" and pulled off the 14-3 upset.

Like coach Frank Leahy, you know the importance of prepa-ration in your own life. You went to the bank for a car loan, facts and figures in hand. That presentation you made at work was seamless because you practiced. The kids' school play suffered no meltdowns because they rehearsed. Knowing what you need to do and doing what you must to succeed isn't luck; it's preparation.

Jesus understood this, and he prepared his followers by lecturing them and by sending them on field trips. Two thousand years later, the life of faith requires similar training and study. You prepare so you'll be ready when that unsaved neighbor standing beside you at your backyard grill asks about Jesus. You prepare so you will know how God wants you to live. You prepare so you are certain in what you believe when the secular, godless world challenges it.

And one day you'll see God face to face. You certainly want to be prepared for that.

We looked across the field and the sun was beating down where we would have been.
 — *Joe McArdle on Frank Leahy's preparation for the '52 Texas game*

**Living in faith requires constant study
and training, preparation for the day
when you meet God face to face.**

WINNER'S CIRCLE

Read 1 John 5:1-12.

"Who is it that overcomes the world? Only he who believes that Jesus is the Son of God" (v. 5).

In the grand scheme of Notre Dame football, the 28-7 defeat of Wake Forest on Nov. 14, 2015, won't be remembered as being all too important. With the win, however, the senior class made history and established its place in Fighting Irish lore.

Minutes before the team took the field, head coach Brian Kelly reminded his team of what was at stake in a contest Notre Dame figured to win rather easily — and did. His called his squad "Team 127" since 2015 was the 127th season of Notre Dame football. He noted that the seniors would be honored in the last game they would play as a unit at home and that this game had monumental significance for them.

Then the Irish went out and won, jumping out to a 21-0 lead ten minutes before halftime. Quarterback DeShone Kizer ran for one score, sophomore defensive lineman Andrew Trumbetti lugged an interception 28 yards for a touchdown, and freshman Josh Adams ripped off a 98-yard touchdown run, the longest run and play in Notre Dame history. Game over.

As Sports Information Director John Heisler put it, "The final numbers were nothing to write home about," but what the game meant to the 28 members of the Class of 2015-16 certainly was. In the locker room, Kelly pointed out to his kneeling players the magnitude of what they had just accomplished.

"There are a lot of players who have been in this locker room, a lot of great teams over the decades, All-Americans and national championship teams," he said. "And this senior class just became the all-time winningest class" in Notre Dame Stadium history. The senior class went 21-3 at home over its four seasons.

After the post-game gathering, the seniors returned to the field for a group photo and — appropriately enough — a victory lap.

Life itself, like college football, is an intense competition. You vie against other job applicants. You seek admission to a college with a limited number of open spots. You compete against others for a date. Sibling rivalry is real; just ask your brother or sister.

Inherent in any competition or in any situation that involves wining and losing is an antagonist. You always have an opponent to overcome, even if it's an inanimate video game, a golf course, or even yourself.

Nobody wants to be numbered among life's losers. We recognize them when we see them, and maybe mutter a prayer that says something like, "There but for the grace of God go I."

But one adversary will defeat us: Death will claim us all. We can turn the tables on this foe, though; we can defeat the grave. A victory is possible, however, only through faith in Jesus Christ. With Jesus, we have hope beyond death because we have life.

With Jesus, we win. For all of eternity.

You've left a legacy.
— Brian Kelly to the winningest senior class in ND Stadium history

Death is the ultimate opponent;
Jesus is the ultimate victor.

THE BIG TIME

Read Revelation 21:22-27; 22:1-6.

"They will see his face, and his name will be on their foreheads. . . . And they will reign for ever and ever" (vv. 22:4, 5c).

In 1909, Notre Dame football changed forever. The Irish hit the big time.

The perception in the early days of college football was that nobody played big-time ball except the schools in the East and perhaps Michigan. After opening the season with three easy wins, the Notre Dame team found itself at a pivotal moment in the program's history. Next up was "the most important two weeks in the pre-Rockne era," a trip east to play Pittsburgh and then a game against Michigan in Ann Arbor. If the Irish could win them both, they could gain the national recognition that had so far eluded them.

The Irish beat Pittsburgh 6-0, in a game that "was a revelation to the Pittsburgh fans, who were surprised to find the Westerners adept at the modern game." Despite being shocked at the loss, the Pitt fans politely applauded the winners when the game ended.

The game featured a 45-yard penalty against the Irish! After being ejected, quarterback Pete Dwyer told an official he "was going to smash him in the mouth and promptly did." The penalty that resulted was half the distance to the goal line: 45 yards. The Irish protested that the only rule in the book covered one player hitting another, that officials didn't count. To no one's surprise, that argument didn't win any favors from the refs.

The Michigan game turned on a blocked field goal attempt. Notre Dame led only 5-3 at the time and went on to win 11-3. The Michigan head coach tried to dismiss the loss as merely a practice game, but his rhetoric was roundly dismissed as sour grapes.

The student body knew the significance of the wins. They threw a victory party that included a bonfire and speeches from school officials praising the team.

We often look around at our current situation and dream of hitting the big time as Notre Dame did. We might look longingly at that vice-president's office or daydream about the day when we're the boss, maybe even of our own business. We may scheme about ways to make a lot of money, or at least more than we're making now. We may even consciously seek out fame and power.

Making it big is just part of the American dream. It's the heart of that which drives immigrants to leave everything they know and come to this country.

The truth, though, is that all of this so-called "big-time" stuff we so earnestly cherish is actually only small potatoes. If we want to speak of what is the real big-time, we better think about God and his dwelling place in Heaven. There we not only see God and Jesus face to face, but we reign. God puts us in charge.

Notre Dame, by defeating Michigan so decisively, earned the right to be ranked with . . . the leading aspirants for the title in this section.
— Chicago Tribune *after the defeat of Michigan in 1909*

Living with God, hanging out with Jesus,
and reigning in Heaven — now that's big time.

HOPE CHEST

Read Psalm 42.

"Put your hope in God, for I will yet praise him, my Savior and my God" (v. 5b).

Haley Scott DeMaria knows that hope can be sorely tested."

On Jan. 24, 1992, the Notre Dame women's swimming team was returning from a meet near Chicago when the bus crashed and overturned four miles from campus in a snowstorm. Two 19-year-old freshman swimmers were killed. Haley Scott, 18 and a freshman, was on that bus.

Most of the other survivors were injured, but it was Scott who was most seriously hurt. Despite a broken back, she managed to pull herself from the wreckage. "All I knew was that I was cold and my back hurt," she said about the hour she lay in the snow.

After two operations, the doctors delivered the bad news: Scott would never walk or swim again. What followed is a story of hope and recovery so remarkable that DeMaria (She married in 2000.) was asked to deliver Notre Dame's 2012 commencement address.

Five days after the accident, she wiggled her right big toe. Like a baby, she soon rolled on a mat and then crawled. Within a month, she cast aside her walker and cane and walked on her own.

She returned to classes at Notre Dame that fall and graduated only one semester behind her classmates. But the rehabilitation was long and ever painful. In the summer of 1992, for instance, rods inserted to keep her spine straight broke through the skin.

She endured three more complex and risky surgeries.

Perhaps most incredible of all, in October 1993, she went back into the water and won her heat in a 50-yard freestyle race.

What gave DeMaria the hope to keep going during the long struggle when it would have been so easy to give up? Two things, she has said: her faith and her desire to honor her fallen teammates.

Only when a life has no hope does it become not worth the living. To hope is not merely to want something; that is desire or wishful thinking. To produce hope, desire must be coupled with some degree of expectation.

Therein lies the great problem. We may wish for a lot of money, relief from our diabetes, or a weight-loss diet that includes all the doughnuts, cheeseburgers, and fried chicken we can devour. Our hopes, however, must be firmly grounded, or they will inevitably lead us to disappointment, shame, and disaster. In other words, false hopes ruin us.

One of the most basic issues of our lives, therefore, becomes discovering or locating that in which we can confidently place our hope. Where can we find sure promises for a future that we can count on? Where can we place our hope with realistic expectations that we can live securely even though some of the promises we rely on are yet to be delivered?

Exactly where Haley Scott DeMaria put her hope: in God. In God and God alone lies our hope.

Keep praying. God listens.
— *Haley Scott DeMaria on the source of her hope*

**God and his sustaining power are the source of
the only meaningful hope possible in our lives.**

DAZED & CONFUSED

Read Genesis 11:1-9.

"There the Lord confused the language of the whole world" (v. 9a).

The end of the 1961 Notre Dame-Syracuse game was so confusing that both sides claimed victory.

Ranked tenth in the nation, the Orangemen scored late to take a 15-14 lead. A scramble by Irish quarterback Frank Budka and a pass to George Sefcik moved the ball to the Syracuse 39 with three seconds left. Joe "the Toe" Perkowski trotted out to attempt what was obviously a preposterous 56-yard field goal.

He squibbed it, and Syracuse fans rushed the field to celebrate their victory. That's when total confusion took over.

Syracuse was called for roughing the kicker. Under the rules of the day, as soon as a kicker booted the ball, a change of possession occurred. This meant that the penalty was on the offensive team because Perkowski had obviously kicked the ball before being knocked down. Since a game can end on an offensive penalty and the clock had run down to zero, Syracuse seemed to have the win.

After some consultation, though, the refs enforced a 15-yard penalty and determined that Perkowski would get another try, this one from 41 yards out. This time, Perkowski was true. Now Notre Dame seemed to have the win at 17-15.

The confusion continued long after the game was over when Syracuse's athletic director got back home and claimed his team had actually won the game. The chiefs of the conferences that had supplied the officials piped up, asserting that the second kick was illegal, the result of a "misinterpretation of the rules." Papers throughout the East clamored for Notre Dame to give up the win.

Notre Dame's president said the university would abide by the decision of the NCAA rules committee. When it refused to review the matter, Syracuse gave up the fight. The win was Notre Dame's.

Though it sometimes doesn't seem that way, confusion is not the natural order of things. God's universe — from the brilliant arrangement of DNA to the complex harmony of a millipede's legs to the dazzling array of the stars — is ordered. God's act of creation was at its most basic the bringing of order out of chaos.

So why then is confusion so pervasive in our society today? Why do so many of us struggle to make sense of our lives, foundering in our confusion over everything from our morals and values to our sexual orientation and our sense of what is right and what is wrong? The lesson of the Tower of Babel is instructive. That which God does not ordain he does not sustain. Thus, confusion is not the problem itself but is rather a symptom of the absence of God's will and God's power in our lives.

For the children of God, confusion manifests itself in a sense of purposelessness. It fills the void created by a lack of intimacy with God. There is nothing confusing about being close to God.

There's the kick. And it is no good! . . . There's the kick! It's high enough. Is it through? It's good!
    — Radio announcer Jim Gibbons on Joe Perkowski's two kicks

**In our lives, keeping confusion away
requires keeping God near.**

DAY 33

STORY TIME

Read Luke 8:26-39.

"'Return home and tell how much God has done for you.'
So the man went away and told all over town how much
Jesus had done for him" (v. 39).

The star-studded national champions of 1946 found their inspiration in the story and example of a third-team guard.

After a 33-0 steamrolling of Pittsburgh in the season's second game, head coach Frank Leahy was furious. He complained about player after player to the press. Finally, one reporter asked if anyone had played well. "Yes," Leahy answered. "Bob McBride."

McBride had three standout seasons at right guard for Leahy before he joined the Army in the spring of 1943. In December 1944, McBride and some fellow soldiers were taken prisoner by the Germans. For thirteen days, they slogged on frozen feet through snow and mud to a prisoner camp. When the last German offensive of the war collapsed, they were moved again; this time they marched for fifty days alongside the German retreat.

McBride had played at Notre Dame at a burly, muscular 210 pounds. Now, though, as he survived on a starvation diet in a POW camp for 123 days, he shriveled.

On April 23, 1945, American troops arrived at the camp. The first doctor to find McBride had studied pre-med at Notre Dame and asked him if he were related to the man who had played football for the Irish. McBride's reply — "I'm him" — astonished the doctor, who couldn't believe that the gaunt figure before him weighing about 90 pounds was the same man.

Doctors said McBride would never play football again, but over the summer of 1946 he worked construction and ate nonstop. He gained up to 180 pounds and returned to school and to the team. He was still too light to start, but after the 1946 season, Assistant Publicity Director Charlie Callahan made sure the list of monograms included one third-string guard: Bob McBride.

So you didn't survive time as a prisoner of war or serve as a team's inspiration at Notre Dame. You nevertheless have a story to tell; it's the story of your life and it's unique. No one else among the billions of people on this planet can tell the same story.

Part of that story is your encounter with Jesus. It's the most important chapter of anyone's life, but all too often believers in Jesus Christ don't tell it. Otherwise brave and daring Christian men and women who wouldn't think twice about skydiving or whitewater rafting often quail when faced with the prospect of speaking about Jesus to someone else. It's the dreaded "W" word: witness. "I just don't know what to say," we sputter.

But witnessing is nothing but telling your story. No one can refute it; no one can claim it isn't true. You don't get into some great theological debate for which you're ill prepared. You just tell the beautiful, awesome story of Jesus and you.

[Bob] McBride was an inspiration for his teammates, who admired his unyielding determination to succeed.
— *Michael Rodio, Notre Dame Class of 2012*

We all have a story to tell, but the most important part of all is the chapter where we meet Jesus.

HAVE A NICE DAY

Read Psalm 34.

"Whoever of you loves life and desires to see many good days, keep your tongue from evil and your lips from speaking lies" (vv. 12-13).

Notre Dame's first full-time football coach was hoping his team wouldn't get waxed too badly. He wound up with one of the best days in Irish football history, one that changed college football.

In the spring of 1913, coach Jesse Harper pondered how to put Irish football on the national map. To that end, he wrote West Point officials about a game. To his surprise, they replied they had an open date on Nov. 1 and would guarantee the school $1,000.

Finances were so tight that Harper took only eighteen players and fourteen sets of cleats on the 718-mile train trip to New York. Most folks agreed it was a fool's errand, this notion of an upstart program like Notre Dame taking on Army.

Army had scouted Notre Dame's 62-0 rout of Alma on Oct. 25. They saw a power running game, and that's what they prepared for. It would be a cakewalk for the larger Army team; at 210 lbs., Irish fullback Ray Eichenlaub was bigger than any of his linemen.

But Harper had a big surprise for the Cadets. Quarterback Gus Dorais and end Knute Rockne had spent the summer as lifeguards. In their idle time, they had practiced throwing the football.

Games of the day were still won "with brute strength and line plunges." Until Nov. 1, 1913, when Notre Dame "threw it cleverly, threw it often, and totally confounded" Army's defense. Dorais completed 14 of 17 passes for 243 yards and two touchdowns. The Irish shocked the helpless Cadets 35-13. The win "spread the school's name across the country." It also changed the college game because it introduced passing as a viable offensive option.

The good day wasn't over. On the way home, a railroad station agent mistook the Irish for Syracuse's football team. They enjoyed a big breakfast — on Syracuse.

It's commonplace today. Someone performs a service for you — a counter clerk, a waiter, a porter — and their parting shot is a cheerful, "Have a nice day!" It's the world's wish for us as if it is the culmination of everything the world has to offer.

For those who put their faith and their trust in the world, it is. They can't hope for anything better because they turn to an inadequate source.

There is something much better, however, than a mere "nice" day. It's a "blessed" day. It's a day that, as the psalmist envisions it, is much more than simply managing to make it through twenty-four hours without a catastrophe or heartbreak. It's a day in which God manifests his goodness by pouring out blessings upon us.

How do we transform a routine "nice" day into an awesome "blessed" day? We trust and obey almighty God rather than the machinations and the people of this world. For God, having a nice day simply isn't good enough. For us, it shouldn't be either.

I was just happy we were going to come out $83 ahead on the deal.
— Coach Jesse Harper on the 1913 Army game

The world offers a nice day;
God offers a blessed day.

FAMILY TIES

Read Mark 3:31-35.

"[Jesus] said, 'Here are my mother and my brothers! Whoever does God's will is my brother and sister and mother'" (vv. 34-35).

Kelly Tripucka earned the nickname "The Master of Disaster" for his physical style of play on the court. Blame it on his family.

Tripucka is one of Notre Dame's greatest basketball players. From 1977-81, he was a four-year starter at small forward and shooting guard for teams that went a combined 92-28. The 1978 team reached the Final Four. As a senior, Tripucka led the 1981 team in both scoring and rebounding. He was named to various All-America teams three times.

Standing 6'6" and weighing 220 lbs., Tripucka was "like a fullback in football," declared his head coach, Digger Phelps. In other words, Tripucka's style of play was not based on daintiness and finesse. It was natural to him, developed in his backyard.

Kelly was the next-to-the-youngest of six boys, the sons of Frank Tripucka, who started at quarterback for Notre Dame in 1948. All six boys played college sports. The lone girl, Heather, came along too early for interscholastic competition. She did, however, once score 56 points in an intramural basketball game.

Dad put up a backboard in the yard and installed lights so the kids could play at night. "Some fathers will teach their kids to bat a ball or to shoot baskets, but I never did that," Frank said. "I just gave them the equipment and let them play."

As the boys got bigger, the games got rougher. "There wasn't a game that didn't end up in a fight," Kelly recalled. Mark, the smallest and the strongest of the Tripucka boys, "sort of scared me," Kelly said. "He'd beat us up and punch us like he hated us."

When the fights broke out, Frank would "come off the porch with a baseball bat or an iron rake . . . [and] whack everybody." Kelly's mom, Randy said, quite sensibly, "You couldn't reason with that many boys trying to kill each other."

Life and the games were quite physical in the Tripucka family.

Some wit said families are like fudge, mostly sweet with a few nuts. You can probably call the names of your sweetest relatives, whom you cherish, and of the nutty ones too, whom you mostly try to avoid at a family reunion. Like it or not, you have a family, and that's God's doing. God cherishes the family so much that he chose to live in one as a son, a brother, and a cousin.

One of Jesus' more radical actions was to redefine the family. No longer is it a single household of blood relatives or even a clan or a tribe. Jesus' family is the result not of an accident of birth but rather a conscious choice. All those who do God's will are members of Jesus' family.

What a startling and downright wonderful thought! You have family members out there you don't even know who stand ready to love you just because you're part of God's family.

We weren't the Waltons and it wasn't all lovey-dovey.
— *Randy Tripucka*

For followers of Jesus, family comes not from a shared ancestry but from a shared faith.

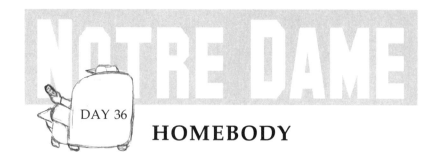

HOMEBODY

Read 2 Corinthians 5:1-10.

"We . . . would prefer to be away from the body and at home with the Lord" (v. 8).

Byron Cobbins was a real homebody while he was at Notre Dame, which was kind of strange since South Bend was 485 miles from his home. The fact that he was mistakenly arrested on a recruiting trip kept him even that close to home.

As a senior linebacker in 1996, Cobbins was a third-team All-America and a team captain. He led the defense in tackles, interceptions, and fumble recoveries his junior year. During his time in South Bend, he achieved a well-deserved reputation as someone who didn't get around very much. "I guess I just like to stay home," he admitted. That was true even if "home" was "a closet-sized single room in a dorm."

Cobbins spent most of his Friday nights playing spades or dominoes with fellow linebacker Kinnon Tatum. Sundays he watched pro football and then stopped by the football office. "He checks on us more than Coach [Lou] Holtz does," said defensive coordinator Bob Davie.

Cobbins grew up in Kansas City, Kan., but when it came time to pick a college, he had no chance to stay close to home. None of the Big Eight programs recruited him seriously. He had to turn to distant suitors such as UCLA, Miami, and Notre Dame.

During his visit to UCLA, Cobbins was riding to a party with

FIGHTING IRISH

a couple of players and an alum when police pulled the car over for a missing tail light. When a search uncovered some loaded handguns, everyone in the car, including Cobbins, was arrested. "I can't believe this," Cobbins said. "I come out to visit a school and get arrested! My mom's going to kill me."

The charges were dropped, but Cobbins canceled a trip to USC since it meant he had to return to California. Notre Dame it was, though it wasn't exactly close to home.

Home is not necessarily a matter of geography. It may be that place you share with your spouse and your children, whether it's South Bend or Kansas. You may feel at home when you return to the Notre Came campus, wondering why you were so eager to leave in the first place. Maybe the home you grew up in still feels like an old shoe, a little worn but comfortable and inviting.

It is no mere happenstance that among the circumstances of life that we most abhor is that of being homeless. That dread is a result of the sense of home God planted in us. Our God is a God of place, and our place is with him.

Thus, we may live a few blocks away from our parents and grandparents or we may relocate every few years, but we will still sometimes feel as though we don't really belong no matter where we are. We don't; our true home is with God in the place Jesus has gone ahead to prepare for us. We are homebodies and we are perpetually homesick.

I don't get off campus much.

— *Notorious homebody Lyron Cobbins*

**We are continually homesick for our real home,
which is with God in Heaven.**

THE REVOLUTIONARY

Read Matthew 3:1-12.

"After me will come one who is more powerful than I, ... He will baptize you with the Holy Spirit and with fire" (v. 11b).

Notre Dame's football players once pitched a revolution that left the coaches' families picketing them.

After the 1969 season, the school ended its longstanding ban on bowl games by meeting Texas in the Cotton Bowl. The team returned to the Cotton Bowl the next season and beat Texas 24-11.

In 1971, the Irish were the glamor pick as the preseason No. 1. But as All-American defensive end and Lombardi Award winner Walt Patulski noted, "We knew we were lacking at some skill positions, and [quarterback Joe] Theismann was just too much to replace." Still, the team had an 8-1 record with only a game against LSU left. That's when trouble started brewing.

The players began what amounted to an uprising by voting to turn down an invitation to the Gator Bowl. "There was a lot of sentiment of people wanting to go back home to their families, and the bowl wouldn't really prove anything," Patulski explained. He and fellow cocaptain Tom Gatewood had the unpleasant task of delivering the news to head coach Ara Parseghian.

He was so livid that the players decided to vote a second time. The count was closer, but the decision was the same. Patulksi called it "a disconnection between the coaches and players." The coaches' wives and their children even picketed the players by standing in front of the practice field and carrying signs about going to a bowl. "It was kind of strange," Patulksi said.

But the players stood their ground. The team didn't play in a bowl game, Gator or otherwise.

Throughout recorded history, revolutions on a much grander scale than that of Notre Dame's players in 1971 have changed the world. From France to Russia to America to Cuba, revolutions have swept across the world stage, demolishing the past in the process. Even the Industrial Revolution changed the world.

No revolution, however, has ever had an impact on history to match the one wrought by an itinerant preacher some two millennia ago. As God's prophet, John the Baptist saw it coming and preached it. This revolution was different in that what it sought was an end to rebellion. John's call was for repentance, a revolution of the soul, a change that would lead to living the way God has prescribed rather than rebelling against God's word.

This revolution shattered everything about human history in that for the first time God himself entered that history as a man. The kingdom of Heaven came to Earth in the person of Jesus Christ, a revolutionary such as the world had never seen before and will never see again.

It was free will and we exercised the right to choose.
— Walt Patulski on the players' vote against the Gator Bowl

All man-made revolutions pale beside
the one God wrought when he brought
the kingdom of Heaven to Earth in Jesus.

MYSTERIOUS WAYS

Read Romans 11:25-36.

"O the depth of the riches and wisdom and knowledge of God! How unsearchable are his judgments and how inscrutable his ways!" (v. 33 NRSV)

The Lord works in mysterious ways." That was about the only explanation All-American linebacker Manti Te'o could come up with for Notre Dame's improbable win over Pittsburgh.

On their way to the BCS title game, the undefeated Irish were heavy favorites when they hosted the 4-4 Panthers on Nov. 3, 2012. At one point, though, the day "had turned black and dreary as the home team had fallen far behind, its unbeaten season seemingly finished." But then some Irish determination, a little luck, and the Lord's mysterious ways saved the day and the season.

Pitt led 20-6 after three quarters. "Our team kept fighting, kept playing," head coach Brian Kelly would say after the game. The Irish did just that, rallying with two fourth-quarter scores to tie the score at 20. Quarterback Everett Golson threw touchdown passes to junior wide receiver TJ Jones and senior running back Theo Riddick. When Golson ran the two-point conversion in with 2:11 left, the game was headed into overtime.

The teams swapped field goals in the first extra period. In the second OT, some mysterious stuff happened. First, an Irish back was headed for a touchdown until he fumbled the ball into the end zone. That meant Pitt needed only a field goal to win it, but the kicker inexplicably missed it. Mysteriously, the Irish had two players wearing jerseys with the No. 2 on them on the field. Even more mysteriously, it wasn't called, so the Panthers didn't get a second chance to win the game with a kick from five yards closer.

Golson's quarterback sneak in the third OT wasn't mysterious at all. With it, Notre Dame had a 29-26 win.

People of faith understand that the good Lord does indeed work in mysterious ways. This only serves to make God even more tantalizing because human nature loves a good mystery. We relish the challenge of uncovering what somebody else wants to hide. We are intrigued by a perplexing whodunit such as *NCIS*, and we enjoy a rousing round of Clue.

Some mysteries we encounter are simply beyond our knowing, however. Events in our lives that are in actuality the mysterious ways of God remain so to us because we can't see the divine machinations. We can see only the results, appreciate that God was behind it all, and give him thanks and praise.

God has revealed much about himself, especially through Jesus, but still much remains unknowable. Why does he tolerate the existence of evil? What does he really look like? Why is he so fond of bugs? What was the inspiration for chocolate and coffee?

We know for sure, though, that God is love, and so we proceed with life, assured that one day all mysteries will be revealed.

Through sports, a coach can offer a boy a way to sneak up on the mystery of manhood.
— *Writer Pat Conroy*

God keeps much about himself shrouded in mystery, but one day we will see and understand.

ALL IN

Read Mark 12:28-34.

"Love the Lord your God with all your heart and with all your soul and with all your mind and with all your strength" (v. 30).

Jewell Loyd wanted to play basketball so badly that she once took on a pair of college kids to gain the use of the court. She was in middle school.

Loyd turned pro after her junior season of 2014-15, leaving Notre Dame as one of its greatest players ever. She was a two-time first-team All-America and in 2015 was named the ACC Player of the Year and *espnW*'s National Player of the Year. She scored 772 points in 2014-15, four shy of the school record for a season set by Katryna Gaither in 1996-97. Her career average of 17.0 points per game ranks second in school history behind Irish associate coach Beth Morgan Cunningham's 18.6 (1993-97).

Her brother, Jarryd, knows what has always driven his sister to excellence. "Her passion [for the game] makes her special," he once said. Simply put, Jewell Loyd loves the game.

The elder sibling learned that lesson one day when he took his middle-school sister to a park down the street from their home. The park had two half courts, and two college kids showed up and tried to kick the Loyds off the court so they could have it. Jewell had no intentions of leaving. She walked right up to the college kids and announced, "We'll play you two on two for the court." The chortling guys agreed; the Loyds beat them 10-2.

That park was a place for serious hoops only, a place "where bruises and bloody noses" were part of every game and rebounds came complete with an elbow to the face.

Loyd never shied away, her passion driving her to the park. "You bleed, wrap it up," she said. "You don't come out." So did the physical games dampen her zeal for basketball? Hardly. "The Final Fours I've played in, the Tennessee games . . . the park games are [still] the most exciting," she said.

What fills your life, your heart, and your soul so much that you sometimes just can't help what you do? We all have zeal and enthusiasm for something, whether it's Fighting Irish football, sports cars, our family, scuba diving, or stamp collecting.

But do we have a zeal for the Lord? We may well jump up and down, scream, holler, even cry — generally making a spectacle of ourselves — when Notre Dame scores. Yet on Sunday morning, if we go to church at all, we probably sit there showing about as much enthusiasm as we would for a root canal.

Of all the divine rules, regulations, and commandments we find in the Bible, Jesus made it crystal clear which one is number one: We are to love God with everything we have. All our heart, all our soul, all our mind, all our strength.

If we do that, our zeal and enthusiasm will burst forth. Like Jewell Loyd and basketball, we just won't be able to help ourselves.

She always wanted to be around basketball.
— Jarryd Loyd on his sister, Jewell

The enthusiasm with which we worship God
reveals the depth of our relationship with him.

DAY 40

JUGGERNAUT

Read Revelation 20.

"Fire came down from heaven and devoured them. And the devil, who deceived them, was thrown into the lake of burning sulfur, where the beast and the false prophet had been thrown" (vv. 9b-10a).

In 1957, Notre Dame took on the greatest juggernaut in college football history — and beat it.

The Irish were big underdogs against the Oklahoma Sooners in Norman on Nov. 16, 1957. The Fighting Irish weren't that bad; they would finish the season 7-3 and in the top ten. It's just that Oklahoma was that good. The Sooners had won 47 straight games, still the longest streak in major college football history.

But Irish head coach Terry Brennan had spotted a weakness he hoped to exploit in taking down the juggernaut. "When you have great success as Oklahoma did, there's a tendency to keep on doing what you're doing," Brennan said. What OU was doing was running the same five plays repeatedly. "Sometimes they set up in different formations, but they were running five plays."

Knowing his defense couldn't dominate the Sooners in head-to-head matchups, Brennan had his linemen attack the gaps rather than the blockers. This would make it easier for them to get into the backfield and wreak some havoc. The risky strategy worked. With twelve minutes left, the game was scoreless.

Notre Dame sat 80 yards away "from football destiny." Full-

FIGHTING IRISH

back Nick Pietrosante and halfbacks Dick Lynch and Frank Reynolds hammered their way downfield on a punishing drive. On fourth down from the OU 3, quarterback Bobby Williams faked a handoff and pitched to Lynch, who scored untouched with just under four minutes to play. The 7-0 score stood up.

Irish cocaptain Ed Sullivan noted that the Sooner fans were so surprised that they didn't begin to leave their seats for nearly twenty minutes after the game ended. They just couldn't believe the Irish had stopped the juggernaut.

Maybe your experience with a juggernaut involved a game in high school against a team loaded with major college prospects, a league tennis match against a former college player, or your presentation at work for a project you knew wasn't going to be approved. Whatever it was, you've been slam-dunked before.

Being part of a juggernaut is certainly more fun than being in the way of one. Consider, for instance, the forces of evil aligned against God. When the Irish took the field that great day in Norman, they had hopes of winning. No such hope exists for those who oppose God.

That's because their fate is already spelled out in detail. It's in the book; we all know how the story ends. God's enemies may talk big and bluster now, but they will be soundly trounced and routed in the most decisive defeat of all time.

You sure want to be on the winning side in that one.

A three-touchdown underdog, no one expected much from Notre Dame.
— Writer Joe Garner on the '57 Oklahoma game

The most lopsided victory in all of history
will be God's ultimate triumph over evil.

DISASTER AREA

Read Luke 21:5-11, 25-28.

"There will be great earthquakes, famines and pestilences in various places, and fearful events and great signs from heaven" (v. 11).

Only a late touchdown kept the opening of renovated Notre Dame Stadium from being an unmitigated disaster.

Irish athletic director Moose Krause once wrote a letter to an alum declaring he shouldn't worry because the expansion of the stadium wasn't too far away. That was some time before Krause retired — in 1981. The expansion to 80,795 seats was not completed until the 1997 season opener against Georgia Tech on Sept. 6.

Everything did not go smoothly that day. The troubles started when thousands of fans without tickets showed up to party in the parking lots. The resulting traffic jam "was the worst in thirty years," according to South Bend police. A minor glitch occurred when the band's PA announcer called for a moment of silence to observe "the recent death of Princess Grace" of Monaco rather than for Diana, Princess of Wales.

Then came the real disaster. What was later deemed to be "a combination of design flaws, low water pressure, and outdated commodes" led to a toilet fiasco of the highest magnitude. Water from dozens of overflowing toilets wound up ankle deep in some places. That led the county health department to close down fifteen concession stands. It also led to $4 million in repairs and lawsuits that took four years to clear up.

The weather didn't cooperate at all. The day turned so muggy that about 150 people had to be treated for heat exhaustion.

The Yellow Jackets didn't help either as the three-touchdown underdogs refused to roll over and die as they were supposed to. Irish halfback Autry Denson scored from the 1 with 2:37 left to avert a total disaster. The score pushed the Irish to a 17-13 win.

We inhabit a world that is struck by one disaster after another on a scale much greater than a bunch of overflowing toilets. Earthquakes virtually obliterate an entire nation; volcanoes erupt and change the climate; children around the world starve to death every day. Floods devastate cities and shatter lives; oil pollutes our oceans and seashores. Can we even count the number of wars that are going on at any one time?

This apparently unending litany of disaster is enough to make us all give up hope. Maybe — but not for the followers of Jesus Christ. The truth is that Jesus' disciples should find reassurance of their ultimate hope in the world's constant disasters because this is exactly what Jesus said would happen.

These disasters indicate that the time of our redemption is drawing near. How near is up to God to decide. Nevertheless, this is a season of hope and great promise for those of the faith.

There's a certain amount of anxiety with a project of that magnitude.
— Notre Dame VP the Rev. E. William Beauchamp on the opening of
renovated Notre Dame Stadium

Jesus told us what to do when disaster threatens
to overwhelm us and our world:
'Stand up and lift up your heads.'

WILD AND CRAZY

Read Mark 3:1-12.

"John's clothes were made of camel's hair, and he had a leather belt around his waist. His food was locusts and wild honey" (v. 4).

Mike Sanford did something pretty wild and crazy — and it changed his life and his career.

Sanford joined Brian Kelly's staff at Notre Dame in 2015 as the offensive coordinator/quarterbacks coach. Back in 2006, though, he was an entry-level coach at UNLV on his father's staff. He decided it was time "to leave dad's coaching shadow, branch out, and find his own way."

But just how in the world would he do that? Well, something wild and crazy might help.

In December, the news broke that Jim Harbaugh, who would land at Michigan eight years later, was taking over the Stanford program. Sanford's wife called her hubby with a wild and crazy idea. She thought he should get on a plane that day and fly out to California to talk to Harbaugh about a job.

The two had a connection from Sanford, Sr.'s time as a coach with the San Diego Chargers. So Sanford, Jr., boarded a plane, "armed only with uncertainty, hope, his finest suit, a desire to reunite with Harbaugh, and a few bucks borrowed from dad." His wild and crazy plan was to show up at Harbaugh's press conference and "see if I could grab a couple of minutes of his time."

FIGHTING IRISH

Then Sanford looked up from his seat in the rear of the plane to see — of all people — Harbaugh strolling down the aisle! He panicked and ducked. Harbaugh's appearance "didn't fit my plan," Sanford explained. One phone call to his wife calmed him down. "This is obviously God's plan coming together," she said.

It was. Incredibly, Harbaugh's seat was next to Sanford, who spent the 45-minute flight selling himself. Thirty days later, he had a new job at Stanford, and his career was off and running.

The lives of college coaches, like the games themselves, are often wild and crazy. But ponder the notion that Jesus calls each one of us to a wild, crazy, and adventuresome life, though perhaps not one as bizarre as that of John the Baptist. Why is it, then, that church and faith life often seem so boring to many of us? Why don't Christians lead lives of adventure and excitement?

Many do. Heading into the uncharted waters of the mission field is certainly exciting. Helping the homeless turn their lives around isn't dull at all. Neither is working with youth, teaching Sunday school, entering the chaplaincy for the military, or riding with a Christian biker gang.

The truth is too many of us play it safe. We prefer to do what we want to do rather than what God calls us to do. As a result, we pass on the chance for our lives to be a great adventure story. We may just be common, ordinary folks, but if we truly follow Jesus, there is nothing common or ordinary about our lives.

Every job [I've] had a chance to get came out of that meeting.
— Mike Sanford on the wild and crazy flight to California

We are a bunch of wild and crazy guys and gals
when we truly surrender our lives to Jesus.

DANCING ANGELS

Read Luke 15:1-10.

"There is rejoicing in the presence of the angels of God over one sinner who repents" (v. 10).

On rare occasions, celebrating players may pick up a teammate and carry him off the playing field or the court on their shoulders. Marc Kelly is certainly the only Notre Dame athlete to be carried out of a *theater* in celebration.

Irish head coach Digger Phelps called Kelly "one of my best walk-ons." From 1978-82, he stuck it out all four seasons, playing in 45 games. That was second only to Tim Healy's record of 57 appearances by a walk-on during the Phelps era. His senior year, Kelly was on the traveling squad and earned a monogram.

His basketball career alone ensured that Kelly would gain a fair amount of fame on campus and locally. That didn't account, however, for his appearances on local radio shows and interviews in the *South Bend Tribune*. Or his being borne boisterously out of a local move house.

All that resulted from something that happened his senior year in high school. Kelly was from Los Angeles, and the summer before he arrived in South Bend, he got a phone call from UCLA assistant coach Jim Harrick. He was a technical advisor for the movie *Fast Break*, the story of a high school team that won a championship behind a girl disguised as a guy.

Harrick told Kelly he needed some extras to play the roles of the opposing team. Kelly agreed to do it and even had a scene in which he spoke two lines. He was paid $512.

When the movie came out in South Bend, Kelly and some of his buddies went to see it. At the end of the movie, those friends lifted Kelly onto their shoulders and carried him out of the theater in rambunctious celebration.

Notre Dame just whipped Southern Cal. You got that new job or that promotion. You just held your newborn child in your arms. Life has those grand moments that call for celebration. You may jump up and down and scream in a wild frenzy at Notre Dame Stadium or share a quiet, sedate candlelight dinner at home — but you celebrate.

Consider then a celebration that is beyond our imagining, one that fills every niche and corner of the very home of God and the angels. Imagine a celebration in Heaven, which also has its grand moments.

Those grand moments are touched off when someone comes to faith in Jesus. Heaven itself rings with the joyous sounds of the singing and dancing of the celebrating angels. Even God rejoices when just one person — you or someone you have introduced to Christ — turns to him.

When you said "yes" to Christ, you made the angels dance. Most importantly of all, you made God smile.

When it comes to celebrating, act like you've been there before.
— Coach Terry Bowden

God himself joins the angels in heavenly celebration when even a single person turns to him through faith in Jesus.

FIASCO!

Read John 18:28-19:16.

"But Pilate answered, 'You take him and crucify him. As for me, I find no basis for a charge against him.'"

A future Heisman Trophy winner's recruiting trip to Notre Dame was such a fiasco it's a wonder he wound up in South Bend.

A right end on both sides of the ball and an occasional fullback, Leon Hart won college football's biggest award in 1949. A four-time monogram winner, he never played on the losing side during his time at Notre Dame; the team went 36-0-2 and won three national titles. He was a three-time All-America, and in 1949, he also won the Maxwell Award as college football's best player.

Hart accomplished all that wearing the wrong size shoes. The Irish equipment manager refused to believe the freshman in 1946 when he said he wore a size fourteen shoe. Hart got thirteens instead. "Back in those days, anything larger than thirteens had to be specially ordered," Hart said. "So thirteens it was."

Not surprisingly, a number of schools went all out to get him to their campus — except for Notre Dame. On Hart's recruiting visit to the campus, he took a late train from Pittsburgh and arrived after midnight. No one met him. The coach designated to meet him at the station was ill; Hart had to call him and wake him up. The fiasco continued when Hart was bunked in the less-than-stylish Quonset huts used by the school's ROTC cadets. About three in the morning, a veteran player came in and kicked Hart out of what he said was his bed.

Some honesty the next morning from head coach Frank Leahy and line coach Edward "Moose" Krause soothed over any ill feelings engendered by the shabby treatment Hart had received.

Like Leon Hart's first trip to Notre Dame, some moments in our lives degenerate into fiascoes. Few general messes in history, though, can match the joke that was Jesus' trial. Pastor, author, and preacher Charles Swindoll said of the whole process, "His arrest was a betrayal, and His trials a farce, His convictions illegal and His punishment a travesty of justice." Throughout the whole fiasco, Jesus spoke the truth, acted calmly and with dignity, and trusted in God to work his will.

Thus did Jesus model how we are to behave during episodes of stress and injustice in our own lives. Things will go wrong for us, sometimes horribly and tragically wrong, sometimes comically wrong, sometimes just frustratingly wrong.

What we can rely on during such times is that even in the midst of chaos and confusion, God is on our side and is working for us. Remember that out of the apparent fiasco of Jesus' trial, conviction, and execution came the means for our salvation. All the while, God was orchestrating the whole sordid business for his own purposes. He will do the same with the messy times in our own lives if we trust him without fail.

[Coaches] 'Moose' Krause and Frank Leahy were very honest with [my dad] even if they didn't take very good care of him.
— Kevin Hart on the fiasco that was his father's recruiting trip

**A life that is a total mess is a fertile field
in which God can work to make it all right.**

WEATHERPROOFED

Read Psalm 147.

"[H]e supplies the earth with rain. . . . He spreads the snow like wool and. . . hurls down his hail like pebbles" *(vv. 8, 16, 17).*

Horrible conditions in "The Snow Bowl" didn't stop the Irish from notching one of "the iconic memories of modern Irish lore."

On Nov. 14, 1992, the 8th-ranked Irish hosted No.-22 Penn State and got a field goal on the opening drive. Then everything changed, and "The Snow Bowl" became part of Irish legend. Snow started falling from a squall that had parked itself over the stadium. Playing conditions and footing soon became difficult.

The snow continued into the second quarter as, not surprisingly, the defenses dominated while the offenses had trouble gaining any traction. Notre Dame eked out a pair of field goals while Penn State scored a touchdown. In a crucial play, freshman Bobby Taylor, an All-America in 1994, blocked the PAT.

With conditions improving after halftime, the offenses picked up. Notre Dame kicked a field goal, but Penn State tied it with a field goal and then took a 16-9 lead with 4:25 left. The Irish set up shop at their own 36 after the kickoff and set about the business of launching themselves into Irish legend.

Quarterback Rick Mirer led a drive that battled the Penn State defense and the clock. With 25 seconds left, the Irish faced a fourth-and-goal at the Lion 3. Head coach Lou Holtz called a play from a formation Notre Dame had never run. It worked.

Mirer scrambled and spotted Jerome Bettis for the touchdown with 20 seconds to play. Having already been booed once at home for going for the tie, Holtz went for two and quickly ad-libbed a play on the sideline. This worked, too, when Mirer hit All-American Reggie Brooks for the conversion and the 17-16 win.

Played mostly in terrible weather, "The Snow Bowl" remains one of Notre Dame's most memorable wins.

A thunderstorm washes away your golf game or the picnic with the kids. Lightning knocks out the electricity just as you settle in at the computer to catch up on some work. A hurricane blows away the vacation you had looked forward to.

For all of our technology and our knowledge, we are still at the mercy of the weather, able only to get a little more advance warning than in the past. The weather answers only to God. Rain and hail will fall where they want to; snow will be totally inconsiderate of something as important as an Irish football game.

We stand mute before the awesome power of the weather, but we should be even more awestruck at the power of the one who controls it, a power beyond our imagining. Neither, however, can we imagine the depths of God's love for us, a love that drove him to die on a cross for us.

A winter squall had descended onto South Bend, and snow swirled around the stadium, blanketing the field white.
— TodayinNDHistory.com, *describing conditions for The Snow Bowl*

The power of the one who controls the weather
is beyond anything we can imagine,
but so is his love for us.

DAY 46

I SEE IT!

Read Isaiah 53.

"But he was pierced for our transgressions, he was crushed for our iniquities; the punishment that brought us peace was upon him, and by his wounds we are healed" (v. 5).

Irish coach Randy Waldrum had a little of the prophet in him. He didn't just expect his women's soccer team to win the national title in 2010; he predicted how they would do it.

Since its inception in 1988, Notre Dame women's soccer "has emerged as one of [the school's] most visible and consistently elite programs." Through the 2015 season, the team has earned a berth in every NCAA Tournament since 1993. They have reached the national semifinals twelve times and have been runners-up five times. They won national championships in 1995, 2004, and 2010; only North Carolina has won more.

The program began humbly. The first varsity squad featured soccer club members and former players from the discontinued field hockey program. "Our practice area was a patch of grass that the men weren't using," recalled Margaret Jarc McLaughlin, whose first season was 1989. "It was a lucky day if we had a goal to shoot on."

The team wore hand-me-down uniforms from the men's team and had a road game only when the men traveled to a school with a women's squad. Both teams crammed into a 23-passenger van

FIGHTING IRISH

for the trips. "It was fun and there was a lot of camaraderie with the men's team, but it was not great soccer," McLaughlin said.

It *was* great soccer on Dec. 5, 2010, when Waldrum made his prediction. His team was to take on top-ranked and undefeated Stanford in the NCAA finals. Before the game, the head coach told freshman Adriana Leon she would score the winning goal. In the 63rd minute, she did just that. Notre Dame won 1-0.

In our jaded age, we have pretty much relegated prophecy to dark rooms in which mysterious women peer into crystal balls or clasp our sweaty palms while uttering some vague generalities. At best, we understand a prophet as someone who predicts future events as Irish head coach Randy Waldrum did.

Within the pages of the Bible, though, we encounter something radically different. A prophet is a messenger from God, one who relays divine revelation to others.

Prophets seem somewhat foreign to us because in one very real sense the age of prophecy is over. In the name of Jesus, we have access to God through our prayers and through scripture. In searching for God's will for our lives, we seek divine revelation. We may speak only for ourselves and not for the greater body of Christ, but we do not need a prophet to discern what God would have us do. We need faith in the one whose birth, life, and death fulfilled more than 300 Bible prophecies.

I teased Adriana [Leon[before the game. I said, 'I have a feeling you're going to get the game winner today.'
— Randy Waldrum on his pre-game prediction

**Persons of faith continuously seek a word
from God for their lives.**

CHEAP TRICKS

Read Acts 19:11-20.

"The evil spirit answered them, 'Jesus I know, and I know about Paul, but who are you?'" (v. 15)

Knute Rockne was never averse to using a trick or two to gain an advantage, but he outdid himself in hornswoggling Southern Cal in 1930.

The Fighting Irish were 9-0 and gunning for their second straight national title when they took on the 8-1 Trojans on Dec. 6 in Los Angeles in the season finale. The team interrupted its train ride west with a layover in Tucson for a final workout. The West Coast writers showed up in droves to watch the Irish practice, not knowing that the whole affair was a sham Rockne had set up for their benefit.

Prior to the practice, Rockne had his players switch jerseys and positions. He put the linemen in the backfield and vice versa. Not surprisingly, the workout was one long, bumbling comedy of errors and miscues. The writers dutifully reported that the Notre Dame team was nothing but a bunch of clods. Their backfield was too big and too slow and the line was too small. They collectively wondered what kinds of teams this woebegone outfit had played back East to win all its games. The writers uniformly predicted an easy USC win.

With the media bamboozled, Rockne pulled a trick on his own players. Though he was only 42, the coach was not a well man. Troubled with phlebitis, he was under a doctor's constant care. With everyone looking on, he ordered the trainer, Scrapiron Young, to change the bandages on his heavily veined legs, said the doctors had warned him not to make the trip, and loudly asked Young, "Do you think I should continue on?" The galvanized, panicked players cried out, "Rock, you can't leave us now."

With just about everybody dutifully tricked, Notre Dame won easily 27-0 in the last game Rockne would coach.

Scam artists are everywhere, and they love trick plays that aren't as beneficial to us as those Knute Rockne pulled to gain an edge. An e-mail encourages you to send money to some foreign country to get rich. That guy at your front door offers to resurface your driveway at a ridiculously low price. A TV ad promises a pill to help you lose weight without diet or exercise.

You've been around; you check things out. The same approach is necessary with spiritual matters, too, because false religions and bogus Christian denominations abound. The key is what any group does with Jesus. Is he the son of God, the ruler of the universe, and the only way to salvation? If not, then what the group espouses is something other than the true Word of God.

The good news about Jesus does indeed sound too good to be true, but the only catch is that there is no catch. When it comes to salvation through Jesus Christ, there's no trick lurking in the fine print. There's just the truth, right there for you to see.

I'm finished with you. I'm going to sit in the stands for the second half.
— A trick Rockne pulled at halftime of the '25 Northwestern game

God's promises through Jesus sound too good to
be true, but the only catch is that there is no catch.

DAY 48

I TOLD YOU SO

Read Matthew 24:15-31.

"See, I have told you ahead of time" (v. 25).

Whatever else he said after the game, linebacker Bob Golic certainly had four words for his head coach: "I told you so."

A linebacker, Golic was a unanimous All-America as a senior captain in 1978. His 146 tackles led the national champions of 1977.

Days before the 1978 Cotton Bowl against Texas, Golic landed in head coach Dan Devine's doghouse, not because of anything he did but because of something he said. "I think we are going to beat them soundly," Golic told the press. Then he added, "In my opinion, it won't be a squeaker." His statement furnished first-class bulletin-board material to a team that didn't seem to need any additional help. Devine quickly made it clear to his star that he didn't want to hear anything else out of him.

Golic and some of his teammates may have felt like they were going to trounce the Longhorns, but few others did. Texas was the only undefeated team in major college ball and was ranked No. 1 with a lineup that included Heisman Trophy winner Earl Campbell. The Irish were ranked fifth in the nation with one loss.

The Texas offense drew all the attention, but somebody should have been noticing the Irish defense. Eight starters would play in the NFL; Golic and All-American defensive end Ross Browner would be All-Pros. That defense had a field day against Texas, forcing three fumbles and grabbing three interceptions.

FIGHTING IRISH

The score was tied 3-3 when the Irish rout began with three touchdowns in eight minutes of the second quarter. Safety Jim Browner recovered a fumble, setting up a touchdown run by Terry Eurick. Willie Fry's fumble recovery set up another Eurick scoring jaunt. A Doug Becker interception put the Irish in business again, and quarterback Joe Montana promptly hit halfback Vagas Ferguson with a touchdown pass.

As *Sports Illustrated* put it, "The game was over right there." The Irish coasted 38-10, just as Golic had said they would.

Don't you just hate it in when somebody says, "I told you so"? That means the other person was right and you were wrong; that other person has spoken the truth. You could have listened to that know-it-all in the first place, but then you would have lost the chance yourself to crow, "I told you so."

In our pluralistic age and society, many view truth as relative, meaning absolute truth does not exist. All belief systems have equal value and merit. But this is a ghastly, dangerous fallacy because it ignores the truth that God proclaimed in the presence and words of Jesus.

In speaking the truth, Jesus told everybody exactly what he was going to do: come back and take his faithful followers with him. Those who don't listen or who don't believe will be left behind with those four awful words, "I told you so," ringing in their ears and wringing their souls.

I just had to remind Coach that I was right all along.
— Bob Golic after the '78 Cotton Bowl

Jesus matter-of-factly told us what he has planned:
He will return to gather all the faithful to himself.

THE MAKEOVER

Read 2 Corinthians 5:11-21.

"If anyone is in Christ, he is a new creation; the old has gone, the new has come!" (v. 17)

Shane Walton arrived in South Bend as a scholarshipped soccer player. He left as an All-American cornerback.

Walton was all-state in football as a senior in California, but soccer was really his game. He played on a club team that won a national championship and also played some internationally.

Walton's only football offer came from Fresno State, and when Notre Dame's Mike Berticelli came through with a soccer scholarship, he took it. His agreement with the head coach was that at some point he could give football a try.

As a freshman in 1998, Walton led the Irish soccer team in scoring. He earned All-Big East second team honors. Something was missing, though. He discovered that playing college soccer was just not as much fun as his club soccer experience had been. He decided to give football a try, and Berticelli helped him.

"I don't know if he thought I'd be a good football player or not," Walton said, "but he was actually the guy who spoke to Coach [Bob] Davie and the staff." After a handful of practices, Davie had seen enough; he offered Walton a scholarship.

The makeover from a soccer player to a cornerback wasn't easy. "I basically had to reprogram my entire body," Walton said. He put on 25 pounds of muscle to power the quick bursts needed of a cornerback rather than the duration required for soccer. "That was the toughest challenge," he said.

Walton saw action in nine games in 1999 as a reserve before becoming a three-year starter. As a senior in 2002, he was a consensus All-America, the first Irish player to earn that distinction since Bobby Taylor in 1994. He was a team captain and the Most Valuable Player. This soccer player who made himself over into a football player was the first Notre Dame player to be nominated for the Bronco Nagurski Award as the national defensive player of the year.

Ever considered a makeover? TV shows show us how changes in clothes, hair, and makeup and some weight loss can radically alter the way a person looks. But these changes are only skin deep. Even with a makeover, the real you — the person inside — remains unchanged. How can you make over that part of you?

You do it by giving your heart and soul to Jesus just as you give up your hair to the makeover stylist. You won't look any different; you won't dance any better; you won't suddenly start talking smarter. The change is on the inside where you are brand new because the model for all you think and feel is now Jesus. He is the one you care about pleasing. Made over by Jesus, you realize that gaining his good opinion — not the world's — is all that really matters. And he isn't the least interested in how you look but how you act.

That process took about a year to really transform.
— Shane Walton on making himself into a football player

**Jesus is the ultimate makeover artist; he can make
you over without changing the way you look.**

UNSTOPPABLE!

Read Acts 5:29-42.

*"If it is from God, you will not be able to stop these men;
you will only find yourselves fighting against God" (v.
39).*

Austin Carr was once so unstoppable in the NCAA Tournament that he set a record some insist will never be broken.

Who is the greatest men's basketball player in Notre Dame history? Writer Lou Somogyi has declared that there can be only one answer. "No deep contemplation is required," he wrote. "No hypothetical conjectures are necessary. The answer remains elementary: Austin Carr, Class of 1971."

History bears him out. Carr played at Notre Dame from 1968-71 in what has been called "the golden age of scorers." He was the linchpin that propelled the program to three NCAA tourney berths and a record of 61-24 during his time in South Bend.

The most prolific scorer in school history, Carr averaged 38.1 points per game as a junior and 37.9 points as a senior. He was a consensus first-team All-America and the national Player of the Year in 1971 and still holds practically every school scoring record.

At no other time, however, was Carr as unstoppable as he was on March 7, 1970, in the first round of the NCAA Tournament. In a 112-82 win over Ohio, Carr poured in 61 points. One researcher reviewed the game and determined that had the 3-point shot been around then, Carr would have scored 73 points.

FIGHTING IRISH

Nevertheless, his total of 61 points still stands as the greatest single scoring night in NCAA Tournament history. With the way the game is played today, Carr's achievement is now generally regarded as one of the sport's unbreakable records.

With his team way ahead late, Irish head coach Johnny Dee told Carr, "We've got the game won. I gotta get you out." Carr knew he was only a few points away from breaking the record of 58 points. He told Dee, "I guess I better try to get it then." He did.

Called "the unguardable guard," Austin Carr was stopped most nights only when the clock ticked down to zero.

Isn't that just the way we would like our life to unfold? One success after another in our career, our family, our investments — whatever we tackle. Unstoppable. The reality is, though, that life isn't like that at all. At some point, we all run into setbacks that stop us dead in our tracks. Everyone does — except God.

For almost two thousand years, the enemies of God have tried to stop Jesus and his people. They killed Jesus; they have persecuted and martyred his followers. Today, heretics and infidels — many of them in America — are more active in their war on Christianity than at any other time in history.

And yet, the Kingdom of God advances, unstoppable despite all opposition. Pursuing God's purposes in our lives puts us on a team bound for glory. Fighting against God gets his enemies nowhere. Except Hell.

It's a good feeling to have the record. I'm amazed it has lasted [this] long.
— Austin Carr on his 61 points in the NCAA Tournament

God's kingdom and purposes are unstoppable
no matter what his enemies try.

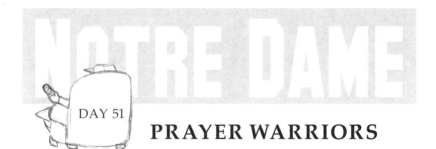
DAY 51

PRAYER WARRIORS

Read Luke 18:1-8.

"Then Jesus told his disciples a parable to show them that they should always pray and not give up" (v. 1).

Nick Rassas prayed for a miracle. His prayer was answered.

Rassas turned down thirteen scholarship offers to walk on at Notre Dame in 1961. For two seasons, he was never promoted past the fifth string. Before the 1963 season he was told in a letter not to report to preseason camp. Only an angry letter from a local priest — he told Irish head coach Hugh Devore he would never get another kid out of Chicago — got him reinstated to the team.

Still, however, Rassas was buried on what amounted to the junior varsity team. As the weeks rolled by in the fall of 1963, he grew more despondent about his chances of playing and considered leaving. His mother had some advice for him. She told her son, "You are being tested whether you believe it or not. Go down to the Grotto and say a prayer."

The next day, Rassas walked to the Grotto, also known as the Cave of Candles, and prayed. He said, "I need some help here. . . . I thank you for everything I have, but I need a break here. Is there any way you can help me here?"

A week later, he was as usual left behind when the squad hit the road for a game. While the team was gone, the scrubs scrimmaged, and assistant coach Brad Lynn filmed it. Rassas ran wild. Lynn put the film canister on Devore's desk and forgot about it.

FIGHTING IRISH

Several weeks later, Devore sat down to watch film of the last game, but put Lynn's film in the projector by mistake. He had never seen anything like the show Rassas put on.

The coach stormed out to practice, blessed Rassas out for not telling him how good he was, and promoted him to first string on the spot. Rassas started the next game and every game after that. As a senior in 1965, he was an All-American safety.

Nick Rassas prayed and didn't give up. That's what Jesus taught us to do as his followers: always pray and never give up.

Any problems we may have with prayer and its results derive from our side, not God's. We pray for a while about something — perhaps fervently at first — but our enthusiasm wanes if we don't receive the answer we want exactly when we want it. Why waste our time by asking for the same thing over and over again?

But God isn't deaf; God does hear our prayers, and God does respond to them. As Jesus clearly taught, our prayers have an impact because they turn the power of Almighty God loose in this world. Thus, falling to our knees and praying to God is not a sign of weakness and helplessness. Rather, praying for someone or something is an aggressive act, an intentional ministry, a conscious and fervent attempt on our part to change someone's life or the world for the better.

God responds to our prayers; we often just can't perceive or don't understand how he is working to answer them.

I need some help here. I pray to you, Our Lady, and hope you can make it fast.
— Nick Rassas, praying for divine intervention

Jesus taught us to always pray and never give up.

DAY 52

HOW WE LEAVE

Read 2 Kings 2:1-12.

"A chariot of fire and horses of fire appeared and separated the two of them, and Elijah went up to heaven in a whirlwind" (v. 11).

When Boston College administrators wouldn't let him leave for Notre Dame, Frank Leahy took matters into his own hands.

Depending on your perspective, Leahy was either a defector or a savior in 1941. His "contentious decision" to leave Boston College and return to his alma mater "sent equal parts angst and joy within the two campuses."

The problem was that Boston College had Leahy and Notre Dame wanted him. After leading the Eagles for two seasons that included the school's only national title, Leahy signed a contract renewal. But when Irish head coach Elmer Layden resigned to become commissioner of the NFL, Leahy begged the BC administration, the mayor of Boston, and the governor of Massachusetts to void his contract so he could leave. They all refused.

Running out of options, time, and patience and passionately wanting the Notre Dame job, Leahy decided to act on his own. He called his own press conference and simply told a big whopping lie to about fifty reporters. He reported that Boston College had voided his contract and he thus would be moving on to coach the Irish. He went so far as to provide the detail that "with the release went the good wishes and benediction of Boston College."

FIGHTING IRISH

Leahy's desperate ploy worked. News of his impending departure quickly circulated all over Boston and South Bend. Backed into a corner, Boston College's vice president begrudgingly telephoned Leahy and officially released him from the contract. The conversation wasn't long or cordial. "You may go wherever you want and whenever you want. Good-bye," the miffed VP said.

On Feb. 15, 1941, six weeks after leading Boston College to the national title, Leahy signed a contract to coach Notre Dame football. Across his eleven seasons, his Irish became a dynasty.

Like Frank Leahy and Elijah, we can't always choose the exact circumstances under which we leave.

You probably haven't always chosen the moves you've made in your life. Perhaps your company transferred you. A landlord didn't renew your lease. An elderly parent needed your care.

Sometimes the only choice we have about leaving is the manner in which we go, whether we depart with style and grace or not. Our exit from life is the same way. Unless we usurp God's authority over life and death, we can't choose how we die, just how we handle it. Perhaps the most frustrating aspect of dying is that we have at most very little control over the process. As with our birth, our death is in God's hands. We finally must surrender to his will even if we have spent a lifetime refusing to do so.

We do, however, control our destination. How we leave isn't up to us; where we spend eternity is — and that depends on our relationship with Jesus.

People were riled when Leahy left.
— The Rev. Charles Donovan, Boston College Class of 1933

How you go isn't up to you; where you go is.

TROUBLED TIMES

Read Nahum 1:1-8.

"The Lord is good, a refuge in times of trouble. He cares for those who trust in him" (v. 8).

The Irish women were in big, big trouble before a pair of rather unlikely heroes bailed them out.

Against third-ranked South Carolina in the semifinal round of the Final Four on April 5, 2015, the second-ranked Irish had about as much trouble as any team could handle. As the last half ticked away, they went 7:35 without scoring. Both point guard Lindsay Allen, the MVP of the regional, and freshman forward Brianna Turner, the team's best shot-blocker and rebounder, fouled out. Then with 1:12 left, South Carolina completed a 13-0 run to take a one-point lead, its first of the game.

The Irish needed a hero; with only 16 seconds left, they got one. Senior reserve guard Madison Cable, who had not scored a point all night, bailed her team out. She "slashed in from nowhere" to grab an offensive rebound and put up "an off-balance, driveway-worthy jumper." There was "nothing smooth or finessed about [the shot]." All it did was go in the hoop. It was nothing more than "a ragged play that won a game."

"That's the kind of shot I've been making since I was little," Cable said. "I crashed the boards when I knew it [would be] short."

Since South Carolina had time to pull the game out, the Irish were still in trouble. They needed another hero. This time it was

FIGHTING IRISH

junior Hannah Huffman, who played only five minutes the entire game. A defensive specialist, she was assigned to guard South Carolina's best bet to take the final shot. It was no contest.

Huffman was all over the shooter well beyond the arc. She deflected a pass that left only enough time for a desperate heave that hit the top of the blackboard. 66-65. On to the NCAA finals.

No trouble at all.

For every Irish basketball team in every game, trouble is gonna come. Winning or losing a game is largely determined by how a team handles the trouble that comes its way during the ebb and flow of the action.

Life is no different. For each of us, trouble is gonna come. The decisive factor for us all is how we handle it. What do we do when we're in trouble?

Admittedly, some troubles are worse and are more devastating than others. From health problems to financial woes to family problems, trouble can change our lives and everything about it.

The most fearsome danger, though, lies not in what trouble can do to us physically, emotionally, or psychologically, but in its potential to affect us spiritually. Do we respond to it by turning to the profane or to the profound? Does trouble wreck our faith in God or strengthen our trust in him?

Like everything of this world, trouble is temporal; God's love and power, however, are not. In God, we have a sure and certain refuge during the troubled times of our lives.

Things couldn't have looked bleaker for No. 2 Notre Dame.
— Writer John Fineran on the South Carolina game

When trouble comes, God will be there for us.

DAY 54

KEEP OUT!

Read Exodus 26:31-35; 30:1-10.

"The curtain will separate the Holy Place from the Most Holy Place" (v. 26:33).

A player who had to argue his way into the stadium played a pivotal role in what many historians still consider to be one of the greatest games of the first half of the twentieth century.

The 5-0 Irish met undefeated Ohio State at Ohio Stadium on Nov. 2, 1935. The Buckeyes led 13-0 headed into the final quarter. The Irish rallied with a two-yard run by fullback Steve Miller and a 33-yard pass from star halfback Andy Pilney to Mike Layden, brother of Irish head coach Elmer Layden. With only two minutes left, the kick for the tie hit the crossbar and bounced away. Ohio State had only to run out the clock for a 13-12 win.

But Pilney caused a fumble with a bone-jarring tackle. Notre Dame got the ball at the OSU 49 with about a minute left to play.

Pilney broke loose to the 19, but suffered a career-ending knee injury on the play. Layden sent in Bill Shakespeare, who would finish third in the Heisman balloting that season. Two plays netted nothing, and Layden needed to send in a play. The bizarre substitution rules forced him to turn to fourth-string quarterback Jim McKenna, who wasn't even supposed to be at the game.

McKenna had been injured in practice that week and thus had not been named to the travel squad. Carrying his uniform, he sneaked onto the team train and hid in a teammate's berth to get to the game. At the stadium, the gatekeepers refused to let him in until he found a sympathetic person who relented.

McKenna sat on the bench, a spectator. Finally, driven to desperation by the arcane substitution rules, Layden had to send him in with a play. He called the signals, took the snap, handed Shakespeare the ball, and threw a perfect block on a heavier Buckeye defender. Shakespeare hit Miller with a strike for a touchdown.

Notre Dame had an 18-13 win, thanks in part to Jim McKenna, who was told to keep off the train and keep out of the stadium.

That civic club with its membership by invitation only. The bleachers where you sit while others frolic in the sky boxes. That neighborhood you can't afford a house in. You know all about being shut out of some club, some group, some place. "Exclusive" is the word that keeps you out.

The Hebrew people, too, knew about being told to keep out. Only the high priest could enter the Most Holy Place — which housed the ark — and survive. Then along came Jesus to kick that barrier down and give us direct access to God.

In the process, though, Jesus created another exclusive club; its members are his followers, Christians, those who believe he is the Son of God and the savior of the world. This club, though, extends a membership invitation to everyone in the whole wide world; no one is excluded. Whether you're in or out depends on your response to Jesus, not on arbitrary gatekeepers.

Up came backfield coach [Chet] Grant, tugging along [Jim] McKenna.
— Writer Joseph Doyle on how Jim McKenna got into the OSU game

Christianity is an exclusive club, but an invitation
is extended to everyone and no one is denied entry.

BEAUTIFUL PEOPLE

Read Matthew 23:23-28.

"Woe to you, teachers of the law and Pharisees, you hypocrites! You are like whitewashed tombs, which look beautiful on the outside, but on the inside are full of dead men's bones and everything unclean" (v. 27).

Joe Theismann decided to play football at Notre Dame because of all the pretty girls. Well, not exactly.

From 1968-70, Theismann rewrote the Irish record book in passing and total offense. As a senior in 1970, he quarterbacked the Irish to a 10-1 season and a No.-2 ranking. He finished second in the Heisman voting to Jim Plunkett of Stanford. The team averaged 510.5 yards per game, a record that still stands. As one writer put it, "Theismann's skill and confidence compensated for the shortage of marquee athletes." That's because not one starting offensive lineman from the 1970 team played in the NFL, and not one of the team's top five running backs was drafted either.

Theismann weighed 152 pounds when he entered college. He was so small that on a recruiting trip to South Bend, defensive coordinator Johnny Ray thought he was a student manager or water boy. Defensive line coach Joe Yonto told him, "No, that's the quarterback." Ray responded, "You gotta be kidding me!"

Theismann was always honest in that academics was not the deciding factor in his choice of a college. "I was a good enough student to get by in high school, but I really wanted to play ball," he said.

One visit to Chapel Hill let him scratch the Tar Heels off his short list. Why? Because of all the pretty coeds he saw. "I'm not capable of focusing with beautiful women around," he said.

Notre Dame, on the other hand, was an all-male institution. Theismann could concentrate on football and his classwork. So that cinched his decision: no beautiful women; Notre Dame it was.

That pretty girl you couldn't work up the nerve to ask out. That hunk who sat behind you in high school. And admit it: Your spouse's looks had a lot to do with your getting married.

Except perhaps for Joe Theismann in college, we do love those beautiful people.

It is worth remembering amid our adulation of and quest for superficial beauty that popular magazines such as *Vogue* or *People* probably wouldn't have been too enamored of Jesus' looks. Isaiah 53 declares that our savior "had no beauty or majesty to attract us to him, nothing in his appearance that we should desire him."

Jesus never urged folks to walk around with body odor and unwashed hair. He did, however, admonish us to avoid being overly concerned with physical beauty, which fades with age despite tucks and Botox. What matters to God is inner beauty, which reveals itself in the practice of justice, mercy, and faith, and which is not only lifelong but eternal.

In God's eyes, true beauty is spiritual, not physical.

I went out on two dates my first two years at Notre Dame.
— *Joe Theismann*

**When it comes to looking good to God,
it's what's inside that counts.**

DAY 56

CHANCE MEETING

Read Luke 24:13-35.

*"That same day two of them were going to a village. . . .
They were talking with each other about everything that
had happened. . . . Jesus himself came up and walked
along with them" (vv. 13-15).*

Chuck Male was just out kicking a football around, unaware someone was noticing. That chance encounter changed his life.

Following the graduation of four-year starter Dave Reeve, Male took over the football team's kicking duties in 1979. In his first game, the senior booted his name into Irish lore. His four field goals accounted for all of the team's points in the 12-10 up-set of 6th-ranked Michigan in the season opener. Male went on to kick thirteen field goals that season, which tied Reeve's record.

That success in an Irish uniform was not easily come by for Male. He grew up a Notre Dame fan, but the school wasn't much of a fan of his; he was denied admission. He enrolled at Western Michigan and was the starting kicker as a freshman. During the year, however, he was accepted at Notre Dame. Rather than stay with the hard-won security he had at WMU, Male decided to follow his dream and head to South Bend.

He had no guarantees, no offers, and no real options. He simply worked on his kicking while he waited for spring practice to begin so he could walk on. But as one writer put it, Male "could have been Rudy." His perseverance in the pursuit of his dream unexpectedly paid off because of a chance meeting.

As he did regularly, Male was kicking by himself one day on Cartier Field. Running on the track, Irish head coach Dan Devine couldn't help but notice this kid across the way booming a football. When he finished, Devine went over to Male and told him, "Go inside and tell [assistant coach] Hank Kuhlman that you're on the team and you need equipment." That was it.

Maybe you met your spouse on a blind date or in the frozen food section of a local supermarket. Perhaps a conversation in an elevator or over lunch led to a job offer.

Chance meetings often shape our lives. Some meetings, however, are too important to be left to what seem like the whims of life. If your child is sick, you don't wait until you happen to bump into a physician at Starbucks to seek help.

So it is with Jesus. Too much is at stake to leave a meeting with him to chance. Instead, you intentionally seek him at church, in the pages of your Bible, on your knees in prayer, or through a conversation with a friend or neighbor. How you conduct the search doesn't matter; what matters is that you find him. After all, he's not in hiding; he's easy to find.

Once you've met him, you should then intentionally cultivate the acquaintance until it is a deep, abiding, life-shaping and life-changing friendship.

Coach Devine would tell people that he 'discovered' me. I felt like I was a continent or something.
    — Chuck Male on his chance encounter with the Irish head coach

A meeting with Jesus should not be a chance encounter, but instead should be sought out.

CHOICES

Read Deuteronomy 30:15-20.

"I have set before you life and death, blessings and curses. Now choose life, so that you and your children may live" (v. 19).

It's pretty safe to say that athletes good enough to earn All-American honors choose the position at which they excel or at least have a coach choose for them. Not John Kemp.

Kemp was a three-time All-American and three-time All-Big East lacrosse goalkeeper at Notre Dame from 2011-13. In 2012 he was the Big East Goalkeeper of the Year. His 36 career wins rank second in school history, behind his older brother, Joey (2005-08). The team reached the NCAA Tournament in each of John Kemp's three seasons in goal. The 2012 squad reached the Final Four.

As the youngest of the seven Kemp children, John wound up with all the hand-me-down clothes. He also served as the test subject for his older brothers' wrestling moves. But being the youngest was also how John found the sport and the position that would eventually lead him to being the first goalie taken in the 2013 pro lacrosse draft.

An older brother gave up baseball for lacrosse because that's what everybody played at his new school. Joey then followed his sibling's path to the cage.

Catholic-school tuition for all the kids resulted in a tight family budget. So when John came along, the household had a

FIGHTING IRISH

bunch of goalie sticks and didn't want to pay for any more sports equipment. "John being the caboose, he wanted to play lacrosse, [and] he got handed a goalie's stick," dad Bob Kemp said.

So John began his lacrosse experience by putting on the pads he wore playing forward in hockey, trotting out to the net in the backyard, and taking target practice for Joey. The choice the youngest Kemp son didn't get to make turned out very well.

Your life is the sum of the choices you've made. That is, you have arrived at this moment and this place in your life because of the choices you made in your past. Even John Kemp at least chose to play lacrosse even if he didn't have much to say about the position he played.

Your love of the Fighting Irish. Your spouse or the absence of one. Mechanic, teacher, doctor, or beautician. Condo in downtown Indianapolis or ranch home in South Bend. Dog, cat, or goldfish. You chose; you live with the results.

That includes the most important choice you will ever have to make: faith or the lack of it. That we have the ability to make decisions when faced with alternatives is a gift from God, who allows that faculty even when he's part of the choice. We can choose whether or not we will love him. God does remind us that this particular choice has rather extreme consequences: Choosing God's way is life; choosing against him is death.

Life or death. What choice is that?

John kinda had no choice.
— *Joey Kemp on John Kemp's playing goalie*

**God gives you the freedom to choose: life or death;
what kind of choice is that?**

BEYOND THE PAST

Read Colossians 3:1-10.

"You used to walk in these ways, in the life you once lived. But now you must rid yourself of all such things" (vv. 7, 8a).

From games against the Chicago Physicians and Surgeons to entire seasons without a head coach, football at Notre Dame in its long-ago past was not exactly like it is today.

Irish football began in 1887 (See Devotion No. 1.) with the first win coming in 1888, a 20-0 defeat of Harvard School of Chicago. The early days were haphazard, to say the least. The 1889 season, for instance, consisted of only one game, a 9-0 defeat of Northwestern. The game was notable for two reasons: The team acquired both its first regular uniforms and a nickname. During the game, Northwestern's students, in what apparently was intended as a religious slur, chanted, "Kill those Irish! Kill those Fighting Irish!"

By then, interest in the sport had declined so much that the school didn't field a team in 1890 or 1891. A shop instructor, James Gilvan, was instrumental in spurring the students to form a team in 1892. Again, the team didn't have a "coacher," as it was called then; instead, the team captain filled the post. A two-game schedule included a 56-0 defeat of South Bend High School.

Irish football took off after that with 21 players participating in 1893. That spurred the school to hire a temporary coach, James L. Morrison, a tackle at Michigan the previous year. He was paid

FIGHTING IRISH

$40 for two weeks, coached one game, and left.

The four-game schedule of 1895 is surely the most bizarre in school history with wins over the Northwestern Law School, the Illinois Cycling Club, the Chicago Physicians and Surgeons, and a loss to a team called the Indianapolis Artillery.

Frank E. Hering, the man some have dubbed the "father of Notre Dame football," arrived in 1896. He was the program's first paid coach as well as the team's quarterback. His pay consisted of tuition plus produce and meat from the school's farm. He gave the program some badly needed stability and direction.

As illustrated by the early days of Nore Dame football, the past often seems quaint to us. But in our personal lives, the past usually isn't quaint at all. Instead, it often haunts us like a ghost. We lug around our regrets and memories of our past failures, omissions, and shortcomings, donning them each day as we do our clothes.

Short of utter callousness and severe memory problems, only one way exists to free ourselves totally from the past: the change offered through salvation in Jesus Christ. Even when we fall on our knees in despair and cry out to Jesus, we sometimes falsely believe that salvation and forgiveness can never be ours. That's because many desperate seekers fall prey to the fallacy that they must be perfect before Jesus will accept them. The truth is that we need Jesus because we are not perfect.

Jesus didn't die for our past but for our future. He died to free us from the past and to replace it with a glorious future.

Make the present good, and the past will take care of itself.
— Knute Rockne

Every saint has a past; every sinner has a future.

DAY 59

PAIN RELIEF

Read 2 Corinthians 1:3-7.

"Just as the sufferings of Christ flow over into our lives, so also through Christ our comfort overflows" (v. 5).

It took Jarrett Grace 22 months to finally play football pain free."

On Oct. 5, 2013, against Arizona State, Grace, a junior Irish linebacker, lay on the turf after a play as he had so many times before. Only this time, he didn't get up. He had suffered what was termed "a devastating injury." "I knew instantly that it wasn't good," he said as excruciating pain swept through him. "I heard a loud snap." In fact, he had broken his right leg in multiple places.

Grace's doctors expected a recovery time of four months. What happened instead was a series of medical setbacks that resulted in a prolonged and painful ordeal lasting for 18 months. Complications from his two surgeries kept Grace in the hospital for nearly a month after the injury.

Fellow Irish linebacker Ben Councell said his roommate never let anyone know the depth of the pain he suffered. He "was in so much pain for probably a year," Councell said. "He wouldn't say anything, but you could see it in his eyes. You'd see it in his walk. But he never complained."

Notre Dame trainer Rob Hunt said Grace was "a profile of courage and determination" during what turned into a "marathon" rehab. Hunt said Grace "handled the emotional and psychological piece probably better than anyone. . . . His commitment to his teammates and to coming back never wavered."

Grace attributed that determination and courage to his faith. "God gives us different gifts," he said. "I was blessed athletically. For me not to pursue that until it's final end . . . would be selling my faith short. If I can get back on the field and share my story in the way God has blessed me, that's a driving factor."

Grace did indeed get back on the field. After missing all of the 2014 season, he was cleared for spring practice. He saw action in every game in 2015 on a squad loaded with linebackers. He finished the season with three starts and 26 tackles.

Since you live on Earth and not in Heaven, you are forced to play with pain. Whether it's a car wreck that left you shattered, the end of a relationship that left you battered, or a loved one's death that left you tattered — pain finds you and challenges you to keep going.

While God's word teaches that you will reap what you sow, life also teaches that pain and hardship are not necessarily the result of personal failure. Pain in fact can be one of the tools God uses to mold your character and change your life.

What are you to do when you are hit full-speed by the awful pain that seems to choke the very will to live out of you? Where is your consolation, your comfort, and your help?

In almighty God, whose love will never fail. When life knocks you to your knees, you're closer to God than ever before.

I like having bruises now. I'll take bruises from football anytime.
— Jarrett Grace on the 'good' pain from playing football again

**When life hits you with pain, you can always
turn to God for comfort, consolation, and hope.**

THE GREATEST

Read Mark 9:33-37.

"If anyone wants to be first, he must be the very last, and the servant of all" (v. 35).

Greatest collection of college football talent in history." So declared *Sports Illustrated*'s Paul Zimmerman about the Notre Dame teams of 1946 and '47. He probably wouldn't get much of an argument from those who know what they're talking about.

Both teams went undefeated and were national champions. The '46 team was held to a scoreless tie by the legendary Doc Blanchard-Glenn Davis team at Army.

The squads not only had the usual assortment of young and talented players, but they were stacked with former starters who had gone off to war and then returned. Six members would be All-NFL. Nine players on the '47 team were All-America at some point. Two of them, Johnny Lujack and Leon Hart, won the Heisman Trophy. Guard Bill Fischer and tackle George Connor won the Outland Trophy as the nation's best lineman. Seven of the players wound up in the College Football Hall of Fame.

Then there were players like Phil Colella, the second-leading Irish rusher in 1945. He had been on two ships sunk by Japanese torpedoes. He came to preseason practice, saw the stockpile of backs on hand, and transferred to St. Bonaventure.

Head coach Frank Leahy's biggest problem was figuring out what to do with all his talent. In 1946, he played his first unit in the first and third quarters and his second unit in the second and fourth quarters. The second unit scored more touchdowns than the first team did.

Determining which players would make the traveling squad was a problem. The solution was two-hour scrimmages in full pads on the Thursdays before road games. That always injured some players, thus making the coaches' decisions easier.

As one writer said about the 1947 team, "The best games [of the season] will be the intrasquad scrimmages at South Bend."

We all want to be the greatest. The goal for the Irish and their fans every season is the national championship. The competition at work is to be the most productive sales person on the staff or the Teacher of the Year. In other words, we define being the greatest in terms of the struggle for personal success. It's nothing new; Jesus' disciples saw greatness in the same way.

As Jesus illustrated, though, greatness in the Kingdom of God has nothing to do with the secular world's understanding of success. Rather, the greatest are those who channel their ambition toward the furtherance of Christ's kingdom through love and service, rather than their own advancement, which is a complete reversal of status and values as the world sees them.

After all, who could be greater than the person who has Jesus for a brother and God for a father? And that's every one of us.

For sheer talent, nothing could match our teams of '46 and '47.
— All-American and Heisman-Trophy winner Leon Hart

**To be great for God has nothing to do
with personal advancement and everything to do
with the advancement of Christ's kingdom.**

MIRACLE PLAY

Read Matthew 12:38-42.

"He answered, 'A wicked and adulterous generation asks for a miraculous sign!'" (v. 39)

Harry Oliver knew he needed a miracle. He got one.

On Sept. 20, 1980, Notre Dame and Michigan battled in one of the most thrilling games in the legendary series' long history. In the third quarter, Oliver missed the PAT after cornerback John Krimm returned an interception 41 yards for a touchdown. That left the score 21-20, and the miss stood up as Michigan led 27-26 with four seconds left in the game.

A five-yard pass from freshman Blair Kiel to tight end Tony Hunter had set the ball down at the Wolverine 34. Head coach Dan Devine bellowed, "Field goal!" Oliver, a left-footed kicker who had tried only one field goal previously, trotted onto the field. The first thing he noticed was that the wind was in his face. The second thing he noticed was that his holder, Tim Koegel and a high school teammate, didn't think he could make it.

When Koegel asked Oliver if we were ready, the kicker replied, "Sure, why?" "Koegel answered, "Because I have a better chance of running this thing in than you do of kicking [it] in there." Then he advised Oliver to kick it hard and kick it straight.

The truth was that Oliver, too, had his doubts. "Honestly, I didn't know if I could do it," he said. He had kicked 65-yard field goals before the game, but he had had the wind at his back. Now, the wind was in his face. If the wind didn't stop, Oliver said, "I didn't have a prayer."

In other words, Harry Oliver and the Irish needed a miracle. They got one. As if on cue, the wind died down. "It was as if Mother Nature got the memo from Touchdown Jesus just in time," wrote Joe Garner.

Bill Siewe made the perfect snap, Koegel laid down a perfect hold, and Oliver hit it like a good golf swing. With the help of a miracle, the 51-yard field goal was good. Notre Dame won 29-27.

Miracles — like the wind dying down before a kick — defy rational explanation. How about escaping with minor abrasions from an accident or recovering from an illness that seemed terminal? Underlying the notion of miracles is the idea that they are rare instances of direct divine intervention that reveal God.

But life shows us quite the contrary, that miracles are anything but rare. Since God made the world and everything in it, everything around you is miraculous. Even you are a miracle. Your life thus can be mundane, dull, and ordinary, or it can be spent in a glorious attitude of childlike wonder and awe. It depends on whether or not you see the world through the eyes of faith. Only through faith can you discern the hand of God in any event; only through faith can you see the miraculous and thus see God.

Jesus knew that miracles don't produce faith, but rather faith produces miracles.

Well, it's miracle time for Notre Dame.
— Announcer Tony Roberts in the closing seconds of the '80 UM game

Miracles are all around us,
but it takes the eyes of faith to see them.

STILL THE SAME

Read Hebrews 13:5-16.

"Jesus Christ is the same yesterday and today and forever" (v. 8).

Notre Dame's basketball coaches once used the future of technology to befuddle UCLA's head coach and to beat his team.

With the possible exception of the 2014-15 Final Eight team, Digger Phelps' 1977-78 bunch may still be the greatest squad in Irish history. They went 23-8 and earned the program's only Final Four appearance. Eight of the first ten players played in the NBA.

Notre Dame assistant coach Frank McLaughlin went to California over Thanksgiving to scout UCLA prior to the game of Dec. 10, 1977. He visited the home of Julian Lobosky, a friend of Phelps', and discovered that Lobosky had a Betamax video recorder in his home. The machines were so new and so rare that the only one back in South Bend at the time was at a local electronics store.

Lobosky agreed to tape three UCLA games and send them to Phelps. The coaches took the tapes down to that local store and spent a full day watching them and taking notes. "In those days," Phelps recalled, "no one had tapes, so you scouted teams in person," which the Irish couldn't do much of with UCLA 2,000 or so miles from South Bend. The tapes thus gave the Irish a big advantage they otherwise would not have had.

They also let Phelps have a little fun at the UCLA head coach's expense. Before the game, Phelps walked up to Gary Cunningham and launched into details about one of the games. He even remarked, "Your tie didn't match that suit the other night."

The perplexed coach knew the Irish couldn't have scouted the game about which Phelps spoke so knowingly, so he had no idea what was going on. Totally prepared, the Irish won 69-66. Before he left LA, Phelps bought a Betamax. Back home, he set up a network of alums across the country to send in tapes of opponents.

The Irish had met the future and it was good.

Like everything else, college basketball has changed since the 1970s. Smartphones, personal computers, ultra-high-definition TVs, cars that park themselves — they and much that is common in your life now may not have been a part of it for very long.

You shouldn't be too harsh on this old world, though, because you've changed also. You've aged, gained or lost weight, gotten married, changed jobs, or relocated.

Change in our contemporary times is often so rapid that it is bewildering and confusing, leaving us casting about for something to hold on to that will always be the same, that we can use as an anchor for our lives. Is there anything in this world like that? Is there anything that is impervious to change?

Sadly, the answer's no. All the things of this world change.

On the other hand, there's Jesus, who is the same today and the same forever, always dependable, always loving you. No matter what happens in our lives, Jesus is still the same.

I was sold on its value. We would have paid $5,000 for it.
— Digger Phelps on the Betamax video recorder

Jesus is the same forever;
his love for you will never change.

DAY 63

DREAM WORLD

Read Joshua 3.

"All Israel passed by until the whole nation had completed the crossing on dry ground" (v. 17b).

Notre Dame wouldn't even give Joe Schmidt a phone call, but that didn't stop him from chasing his dream.

Schmidt grew up in California, and his dad was a fan of the Irish. By the time he was 5, little Joe's dream was to play football in South Bend. Unfortunately, Notre Dame didn't share that dream.

Despite being a high-school star, the best scholarship offers Schmidt landed came from the Air Force Academy, Arizona, and Cincinnati. Notre Dame's coaches had no interest in using a scholarship on an undersized linebacker. That didn't stop Schmidt, however, from pestering them with repeated calls and e-mails.

Head coach Brian Kelly told Schmidt flatly that he was interested in him only as a walk-on. "It was like, 'Joe, we can't call you,'" Kelly said. "He's like, 'Why aren't you calling me? I want to come to Notre Dame.' So we're trying to fend this guy off that we want."

Schmidt's dream won out; he took the difficult route of walking on to the Notre Dame football team in 2011. Predictably, he spent the season on the scout team and never got onto the field. In 2012, though, his dream came true when he played in ten games with the special teams unit.

He played well enough to earn a scholarship before the 2013

season began. On Twitter, Schmidt let everyone know his reaction: "I am so blessed. Thank you God thank you God thank you God."

In 2014, the walk-on who dared to dream became a starter. His teammates voted him the squad's most valuable player. In 2015, Schmidt was named a team captain. One writer noted that if Rudy Ruettiger got a movie, "what will be done with the story of a former walk-on who became not only a starter, but a captain?" Even Kelly admitted, "It's a pretty cool story."

No matter how tightly or doggedly we may cling to our dreams, devotion to them won't make them a reality. Moreover, the cold truth is that all too often dreams don't come true even when we put forth a mighty effort. The realization of dreams generally results from a head-on collision of persistence and timing.

But what if our dreams don't come true because they're not the same dreams God has for us? That is, they're not good enough and, in many cases, they're not big enough.

God calls us to great achievements because God's dreams for us are greater than our dreams for ourselves. Could the Israelites, wallowing in the misery of slavery, even dream of a land of their own? Could they imagine actually going to such a place?

The fulfillment of such great dreams occurs only when our dreams and God's will for our lives are the same. Our dreams should be worthy of our best — and worthy of God's involvement in making them come true.

As a kid, my dream was always to play at Notre Dame.
— Joe Schmidt

**If our dreams are to come true, they must
be worthy of God's involvement in them.**

DAY 64

GREAT EXPECTATIONS

Read John 1:43-51.

"'Nazareth! Can anything good come from there?'
Nathanael asked" (v. 46).

His coach thought he might be "adequate" at tailback, and even he thought he'd be little more than a practice player. Despite those low expectations, Lee Becton became a star on one of Notre Dame's greatest teams.

As a child, Becton had arthritis and a heart murmur, but those infirmities disappeared as he grew up. Despite a great senior season, he was surprised when a Notre Dame scout showed up in Ernul, N.C., to take a look at him. He jumped at Notre Dame's scholarship offer "despite his misgivings about whether he could ever be more than a practice player for the Irish."

Irish head coach Lou Holtz expected little of him, too, especially after his first two seasons on campus. Becton had only fifteen carries as a freshman in 1991 and then spent his sophomore season as a backup to All-American Reggie Brooks. When Becton pulled a hamstring before the '92 BYU game, Holtz quipped, "I didn't think he could run fast enough to pull a hamstring."

Before the '93 season, Holtz "hoped that Becton would be 'adequate' at tailback" while freshman Randy Kinder got ready to take over. Slowed by another hamstring pull, Becton wasn't even adequate against Stanford on Oct. 2, rushing for a mere 25 years.

After that, though, Becton recovered from his injury and had a breakout season. He became the first back in school history to rush for at least 100 yards in seven straight games. The '93 Irish went 11-1, an upset loss to Boston College costing them the national title. Becton finished with 1,044 yards and was the offensive MVP in the Cotton Bowl, a 24-21 win over Texas A&M.

Becton, who arrived in South Bend with few expectations of greatness, finished his career with four monograms. He was only the twelfth back in Irish history to rush for more than 2,000 yards.

The blind date your friend promised would look like Brad Pitt or Jennifer Aniston but instead bore a startling resemblance to Cousin Itt or an extra in a zombie flick. Your vacation that went downhill after the lost luggage. Often your expectations are raised only to be dashed. Sometimes it's best not to get your hopes up; then at least you have the possibility of being surprised.

Worst of all, perhaps, is when you realize that you are the one not meeting others' expectations. The fact is, though, that you aren't here to live up to what others think of you. Jesus didn't; in part, that's why they killed him. But he did meet God's expectations for his life, which was all that really mattered.

Because God's kingdom is so great, God does have great expectations for any who would enter, and you should not take them lightly. What the world expects from you is of no importance; what God expects from you is paramount.

I never think about getting 100 yards.
— Lee Becton on his expectations for a game

You have little if anything to gain from meeting the world's expectations of you; you have all of eternity to gain from meeting God's.

DAY 65

PROMISES, PROMISES

Read 2 Corinthians 1:16-20.

"No matter how many promises God has made, they are 'Yes' in Christ" (v. 20).

Each fall, Notre Dame stays true to a promise that was made decades ago.

The Notre-Dame Navy football series is the longest uninterrupted intersectional rivalry in college football — and one of the most lopsided. Until Navy won a triple-overtime game in 2007, Notre Dame had won 43 games in a row, the longest series win streak between two opponents in the history of major college football. Through 2015, the Irish led the series 76-12-1.

So why in the world does such a one-sided match-up continue? For the Irish, it's payment on a debt of honor.

"We were out of business during World War II," recalled the Rev. Theodore Hesburgh, who served as Notre Dame's president from 1952-87. To alleviate the desperate cash flow problems, the Rev. Hugh O'Donnell, the school president at the time, offered the school's facilities to the armed services as a training ground.

The Army did not respond, but the Navy did. In early 1942, the school turned four of its residence halls over to the Navy for its officers training program. An estimated 12,000 officers completed their training at Notre Dame between 1942 and 1946.

While the Navy and the country benefited from the arrangement, so did the school. "Navy came in and kept us afloat until the war was over," Hesburgh said. The 1943 Irish national title team featured several Navy apprentice seamen and marine trainees, including Heisman-Trophy winning quarterbacks John Lujack (1947) and Angelo Bertelli (1943), Hall of Fame tackle Ziggy Czarobski, guard Pat Filley, and All-American end John Yonakor.

Out of gratitude, Hesburgh promised that under his watch the football series between the schools would continue as long as Navy wanted it to. To this day, Navy has never wanted to end it.

Like Notre Dame's honoring a promise made long ago, the promises you keep tell everything about you.

The promise to your daughter to show up for her softball game. To your son to help him with his math homework. To your parents to come see them soon. To your spouse to remain faithful until death parts you. And remember what you promised God?

You may carelessly throw promises around, but you can never outpromise God, who is downright profligate with his promises. For instance, he has promised to love you always, to forgive you no matter what you do, and to prepare a place for you with him in Heaven.

And there's more good news in that God operates on this simple premise: Promises made are promises kept. You can rely absolutely on God's promises. The people to whom you make them should be able to rely just as surely on your promises.

Despite the one-sided result the last few decades, most Notre Dame and Navy fans consider the series a sacred tradition for historical reasons.
— *Wikipedia, the free encyclopedia*

**God keeps his promises just as those
who rely on you expect you to keep yours.**

THE PRIZE

Read Philippians 3:10-16.

"I press on toward the goal to win the prize for which God has called me heavenward in Christ Jesus" (v. 14).

We are never likely to see a repeat of someone like Notre Dame's Angelo Bertelli winning the Heisman Trophy, college football's biggest prize. That's because he played in only six games the year he won it.

The foundation for Bertelli's win in 1943 was laid years earlier by Knute Rockne. First of all, he agreed to play Army annually in New York City. Then he set up an annual tilt with Southern Cal. That gave the Irish media exposure and publicity from Manhattan to Los Angeles, literally from sea to shining sea.

Frank Leahy was the head man when Bertelli, the son of Italian immigrant parents, arrived at Notre Dame in 1941 to quarterback the coach's T-formation. The Irish went 7-2-2 in 1942, and Bertelli finished sixth in the Heisman voting. The stage was set for the sensational 1943 season.

The Irish rolled past Pitt 41-0 and Ga. Tech 55-13, setting up a huge showdown with second-ranked Michigan. "In the biggest arena in the biggest game, Bertelli was the clear star." The top-ranked Irish won easily 35-12.

Romps over Wisconsin (50-0), Illinois (47-0), and Navy (33-6) followed. Bertelli threw just 36 passes in those six games and completed 25 of them for ten touchdowns, which would be an astounding quarterback rating under today's system.

But then his season ended. Aware of the scourge of Benito Mussolini in his parents' home country, Bertelli had enlisted in the Marines in 1942 and was called to active duty. While others played ball, Bertelli took part in the invasion of Iwo Jima.

In this patriotic time, the nation realized that the duty to put on the military uniform was a higher calling than the duty to wear a football uniform. Bertelli dominated the Heisman voting.

Even the most modest and self-effacing among us can't help but be pleased by prizes and honors. They symbolize the approval and appreciation of others, whether it's something as grand as the Heisman or as simple as an Employee of the Month plaque or the sign declaring yours as the neighborhood's prettiest yard.

Such prizes and awards are often the culmination of the pursuit of personal achievement and accomplishment. They represent accolades and recognition from the world. Nothing is inherently wrong with any of that as long as we keep them in perspective.

That is, we must never let awards become such idols that we worship or lower our sight from the greatest prize of all and the only one truly worth winning. It's one that won't rust, collect dust, or leave us wondering why we worked so hard to win it in the first place. The ultimate prize is eternal life, and it's ours through Jesus Christ.

A gold medal is a wonderful thing, but if you're not enough without it, you'll never be enough with it.
— *John Candy in* Cool Running

**God has the greatest prize of all ready
to hand to you through Jesus Christ.**

DAY 67

FOOD FOR THOUGHT

Read Genesis 9:1-7.

"Everything that lives and moves will be food for you. Just as I gave you the green plants, I now give you everything" (v. 3).

Breakfast on the morning of Oct. 20, 1990, was very good for the Irish football team. The food was okay, too.

In the late 1980s, the Notre Dame-Miami series had come to dominate the college football landscape. Irish quarterback Rick Mirer, who at the time accounted for more points running and throwing (350) than any other player in Notre Dame history, said of the games, "The Miami rivalry brought out the best in us."

The 1990 game of Oct. 20 was the last one. Miami strolled into Notre Dame Stadium ranked second in the country; Notre Dame was ranked sixth. Behind five Craig Hentrich field goals and a 94-yard kickoff return for a touchdown from Raghib "Rocket" Ismail, Notre Dame led 22-20 with less than ten minutes to play.

The Irish faced third-and-four at the Miami 21. Cue breakfast. Over the morning meal that day, head coach Lou Holtz, fullback Rodney Culver, and Mirer drew up and discussed a new play to counter Miami's ferocious pass rush. When Ismail brought the play to Mirer in the huddle, it was the one from breakfast.

Sure enough, Miami sent seven pass rushers on a blitz. Culver faked a block and released over the middle. Mirer looked right and threw back to a spot. Culver cradled the ball, got a crushing

FIGHTING IRISH

block from halfback Tony Brooks, broke a tackle, and scored. The final of 29-20 was on the scoreboard.

The intensity of the rivalry was illustrated when Notre Dame called timeout with 1:42 to go. As the Irish huddled with the outcome not in doubt, the offensive line held hands with tears rolling down their faces. They had opened up holes for 276 yards rushing, more than four times the Canes had been allowing. Mirer and other backs slapped their helmets in acknowledgement.

Belly up to the buffet, boys and girls, for pot roast, sirloin steak, grilled chicken, and all the crab legs you can eat. Rachael Ray's a household name; hamburger joints, pizza parlors, and taco stands lurk on every corner; and we have a TV channel devoted exclusively to food. We love our chow.

Food is one of God's really good ideas, but consider the complex divine plan that begins with a kernel and winds up with corn-on-the-cob slathered with butter and littered with salt. The creator of all life devised a downright fascinating and effective system in which living things are sustained and nourished physically through the sacrifice of other living things in a way similar to what Christ underwent to save us spiritually.

Whether it's fast food or home-cooked, practically everything we eat is a gift from God secured through a divine plan in which some plants and/or animals have given up their lives. Pausing to give thanks before we dive in seems the least we can do.

Rick Mirer helped seal Miami's fate over a plate of breakfast.
— *Writer Jerry Barca on the 1990 game*

God's system nourishes us through the sacrifice of other living things; that's worth a thank-you.

WHAT A SURPRISE!

Read 1 Thessalonians 5:1-11.

"But you, brothers, are not in darkness so that this day should surprise you like a thief" (v. 4).

Notre Dame quarterback Tom Clements was so surprised by the play call that he actually flinched. He had reason to.

Clements led the Irish of 1973 to a 10-0 record and a berth in the Sugar Bowl. The opponent in New Orleans was top-ranked Alabama, and the national championship was on the line.

Leading rusher Wayne Bullock scored from the 1, freshman Al Hunter returned a kickoff 93 yards, Eric Penick got loose for a 12-yard TD run, and Bob Thomas booted a 19-yard field goal with 5:13 left in the game. Notre Dame led 24-23.

The Irish defense held, but a 69-yard punt backed them up to their own 1-yard line. After two runs barely moved the line of scrimmage and the clock stopped with 2:12 left, the Irish coaches faced a big decision. "I think it was the first time that I saw Tom Clements look surprised," said backfield coach Tom Pagna when head coach Ara Parseghian told his quarterback what play to run.

Clements wasn't the only one; Pagna was surprised, too. "I remember asking Ara if he really had called that play," Pagna said after the game. The head coach said he did. "What could I say?" Pagna said. "I told Ara it was a good call."

Clements also wasn't too sure he was hearing his head coach correctly. He asked Parseghian if he was sure he wanted that play.

FIGHTING IRISH

The coach stood firm. Bucking the trend, guard Frank Pomarico, a captain that season, said, "The call didn't surprise me."

What was the call? A pass from the Irish end zone, a play that's commonplace today but wasn't done in 1973. Clements hit tight end Robin Weber for a thirty-five yard gain and a game-clinching first down. Weber may have been as surprised as everybody else; it was only his second reception of the season.

Surprise birthday parties are a delight. And what's the fun of opening Christmas presents when we already know what's in them? Some surprises in life — such as big Irish plays — provide us with experiences that are both joyful and delightful.

Generally, though, we expend energy and resources to avoid most surprises and the impact they may have upon our lives. We may be surprised by the exact timing of a baby's arrival, but we nevertheless have the bags packed beforehand and the nursery all set for its occupant. Paul used this very image (v. 3) to describe the Day of the Lord, when Jesus will return to claim his own and establish his kingdom. We may be caught by surprise, but we must still be ready.

The consequences of being caught unprepared by a baby's insistence on being born are serious indeed. They pale, however, beside the eternal effects of not being ready when Jesus returns. We prepare ourselves just as Paul told us to (v. 8): We live in faith, hope, and love, ever on the alert for that great, promised day.

That pass really caught us by surprise.
— *Alabama assistant Mal Moore*

**The timing of Jesus' return will be a surprise;
the consequences should not be.**

HOMELESS

Read Matthew 8:18-22.

"Jesus replied, 'Foxes have holes and birds of the air have nests, but the Son of Man has no place to lay his head'" (v. 20).

For one season, Notre Dame's football team didn't have a home stadium to play in, so all the games were played on the road. It didn't matter; the Irish had one of their greatest seasons ever.

From 1918-30, Knute Rockne was Notre Dame's head football coach, "athletic director, business manager, track coach, ticket distributor, equipment manager, and uniform designer at various points in between." He was also the school's resident visionary.

What Rockne envisioned was a new football stadium. Since 1900, the Irish had played football at Cartier Field, which was north of the current stadium. With a capacity of about 27,000, it wasn't big enough to attract big-time teams. Under Rockne, football at Notre Dame had become big business. He envisioned it becoming bigger, but he needed a big-time stadium to play in.

Getting that stadium wasn't easy. The powers-that-be were seriously concerned that a new facility would raise doubts about the school's commitment to academic excellence. Some in the administration didn't share Rockne's vision. They reasoned that since the school had only 3,000 students, there simply was no need for a stadium of the massive size that Rockne envisioned.

Threatening to go coach at other schools, Rockne eventually

FIGHTING IRISH

won the day and got his stadium.

Excavation began in October 1929, and Notre Dame Stadium with its 59,075 seats opened for the 1930 season. It came complete with the sod from Cartier that the superstitious Rockne insisted be transplanted. Thus, the 1929 team didn't have a home field and was forced to play all nine of its games on the road. From New York to California to Georgia, the team crisscrossed the country. The homeless and peripatetic Irish went 9-0 and won Rockne's second national title.

Rock bottom in America has a face: the bag lady pushing a shopping cart; the scruffy guy with a beard and a backpack at the interstate exit holding a cardboard sign. Look closer at that bag lady or that scruffy guy, though, and you may see desperate women with children fleeing violence, veterans haunted by their combat experiences, or sick or injured former workers.

Few of us are indifferent to the homeless when we're around them. They often raise quite strong passions, whether we regard them as a ministry or an odorous nuisance. They trouble us, perhaps because we realize that we're only one catastrophic illness and a few paychecks away from joining them. They remind us of how tenuous our own holds upon material success really are.

But they also stir our compassion because we serve a Lord who — like them — had no home, and for whom the homeless, too, are his children.

Almost everyone was sober.
— South Bend Tribune *on Notre Dame Stadium's opening game*

**Because they, too, are God's children,
the homeless merit our compassion, not our scorn.**

DAY 70

CLUELESS

Read Matthew 16:21-23.

"[Y]ou do not have in mind the things of God, but the things of men" (v. 23b).

When she was in the sixth grade, Andrea McHugh broke her dad's heart. Daughter and dad were just clueless, though, about something going on all around them that would change her life.

From 2010-13, McHugh was a four-time monogram winner and two-time captain for the Irish volleyball team. In 2010, she was the Big East Freshman of the Year. She was such a devastating outside hitter that opponents double-teamed their block against her. As a senior, at coach Debbie Brown's request, she moved to the libero slot, a defensive position, and led the team in digs.

McHugh grew up in a family whose activities centered around athletics and their Christian faith. She played every match her junior season at Notre Dame with the word "freedom" scrawled on her hand. Over the summer, she had completed an internship with the Fellowship of Christian Athletes that had focused on playing with freedom, strengthened by God's love.

McHugh's first exposure to competitive sports came with a soccer game when she was five. Looking on was her dad, Jeff, and he was pleased with what he saw. "From the first day," he said, "you could tell she was a natural athlete."

In the sixth grade, though, she dropped soccer and basketball because they were too physical. To her dad's dismay, she took up dancing. "I was devastated," Jeff admitted, at the thought of this exceptionally gifted athlete not playing any high school sports.

But all around the clueless McHugh household was a burgeoning club sport just perfect for Andrea. In the eighth grade, she tried out for a club volleyball team. "She had found a sport she loved," her amazed and once-clueless father said.

"Clueless" is an interesting word in that it is its own oxymoron. People are clueless only when they do have the clues at hand and still don't get it such as Jeff McHugh's unawareness of club volleyball. It's not to be confused with ignorance, which occurs when people don't have access to facts, figures, and information.

From the desert-dwelling Israelites grumbling about Moses and God to the Pharisees and other religious leaders of Jesus' day, the Bible is replete with the clueless. Simon Peter, who had all the clues he needed standing right in front of his face, drew a soul-searing rebuke from Jesus for being clueless.

The Bible remains relevant and timeless because centuries after it was compiled, human nature hasn't changed at all. As it was in Jesus' time, people who have heard the Gospel may still be divided into the clued-in and the clueless: those who get it and those who don't. Fortunately for the clueless, they can always change groups as Peter did. They can affirm Jesus as their savior and give their lives to him. They just need you to clue them in.

Jeff McHugh's head had been buried in the proverbial sand when it came to being clued in about club volleyball right in his own backyard.
— Writer Pete LaFleur, Notre Dame Class of 1990

Clueless or clued-in is a matter
of whether you have given your life to Jesus.

DAY 71

SMART MOVE

Read 1 Kings 4:29-34; 11:1-6.

"[Solomon] was wiser than any other man. . . . As Solomon grew old, his wives turned his heart after other gods, and his heart was not fully devoted to the Lord his God" (vv. 4:31, 11:4).

Irish Head coach Brian Kelly made some unorthodox decisions that turned out to be really smart moves. They netted "one of the most productive running backs in Notre Dame history."

C.J. Prosise's unusual journey to Fighting Irish stardom began not with a touchdown run or catch but with a dunk. He was just fooling around and showing off one day in his high school gym, performing "an impromptu dunk show." Kelly was among those watching. The Irish boss was on a recruiting trip, but not to sweet-talk Prosise, who was "a lightly celebrated three-star recruit."

That all changed when Kelly saw the dunk show. "I saw this athlete," he recalled. "And I said, 'I don't know where he's going to play, but we've got to take him.'"

Finding a place for "this athlete" to play proved more difficult than getting him to Notre Dame. Prosise arrived in South Bend in 2012 as a defensive back. Quickly, the coaches decided that he didn't backpedal very well, so they made the unusual move of shifting him across the line to wide receiver. Prosise spent the next three seasons as a part-time starting receiver and special-teams player who performed well if not spectacularly.

In the spring of 2015, the team was short of running backs, so Kelly made another unorthodox move: He shifted Prosise to tailback. When the starter was hurt in the season-opening win over Texas, Prosise took over. He proved the whole sequence of unusual moves back to high school to be the right ones.

He led the 2015 team in rushing with 1,032 yards and 11 touchdowns. Against Georgia Tech, he set a school record (broken by freshman Josh Adams vs. Wake Forest) with a 91-yard TD run.

Remember that time you wrecked the car when you spilled hot coffee on your lap? That cold morning you fell out of the boat?

Our moves don't always work out as well as Brian Kelly's did with C.J. Prosise. Despite formal education, we all make some dumb moves because time spent in a classroom is not an accurate gauge of common sense. Folks impressed with their own smarts often grace us with erudite pronouncements that we intuitively recognize as flawed, unworkable, or simply wrong.

A good example is the observation that great intelligence and scholarship are inherently incompatible with a deep and abiding faith in God. That is, the more we know, the less we believe. Any incompatibility occurs, however, only because we begin to trust in our own wisdom rather than the wisdom of God. We forget, as Solomon did, that God is the ultimate source of all our knowledge and wisdom and that even our ability to learn is a gift from God.

Not smart at all.

We've just got to find a place for [C.J. Prosise] to play.
— Brian Kelly after he saw Prosise's dunk show

**Being truly smart means trusting in God's
wisdom rather than only in our own knowledge.**

JUST PERFECT

Read Matthew 5:43-48.

"Be perfect, therefore, as your heavenly Father is perfect"
(v. 48).

The idea of any football player having a perfect college career is ludicrous, but if ever such a thing is possible, Leon Hart had it.

Hart was 17 years old when he enrolled at Notre Dame in the fall of 1946. From the start, he was huge. To this day, he remains the biggest Heisman-Trophy winner of all time.

Hart was 6'4" tall and weighed 245 pounds, which was exceptional size for the day. Twenty years after Hart's arrival, Irish great Don "the Hitter" Gmitter started at tight end for the national champions of 1966. He stood 6'2" and weighed 210 pounds.

Hart played tight end and defensive end. On offense, he was primarily a blocker for the featured running game. Still, he hauled in 35 passes for 488 yards and nine TDs his last two seasons.

Not surprisingly, Hart terrorized the opposition's always-outsized defensive backs after he did catch a pass. Head coach Frank Leahy raved that in the 1948 Southern Cal game, "eight Southern Cal lads had their arms around Leon at various times after he caught a short pass from Frank Tripucka, but Leon just ran over them and left them for dead."

Equally frightening for defenses was that Leahy sometimes used Hart at fullback. In 1949, he had 73 yards on 18 carries.

But what about that "perfect college career" blather? Consider this: In what is surely the best career any college football player has ever had, Hart never lost a college football game, his teams won three national titles, he was a three-time All-America, he won the Heisman Trophy (the last lineman to do so), and he was the first pick in the NFL draft after his senior season. Perhaps only a fourth national title and another year of All-America honors kept Hart's time at Notre Dame from being truly perfect.

Nobody's perfect; we all make mistakes every day. We botch our personal relationships; at work we seek competence, not perfection. Indeed, to insist upon personal or professional perfection in our lives is to establish an impossibly high standard that will eventually destroy us physically, emotionally, and mentally.

Yet that is exactly the standard that God sets for us. Our love is to be perfect, never ceasing, never failing, never qualified — just the way God loves us. And Jesus didn't limit his command to preachers and goody-two-shoes types. All of his disciples are to be perfect as they navigate their way through the world's ambiguous definition and understanding of love.

But that's impossible! Well, not necessarily, if to love perfectly is to serve God wholeheartedly and to follow Jesus with single-minded devotion. Anyhow, in his perfect love for us, God makes allowance for our imperfect love and the consequences of it in the perfection of Jesus.

If we chase perfection, we can catch excellence.
— *Vince Lombardi*

In his perfect love for us, God provides a way
for us to escape the consequences
of our imperfect love for him: Jesus.

CLOTHES HORSE

Read Genesis 37:1-11.

"Israel loved Joseph more than all his children, because he was the son of his old age: and he made him a coat of many colours" (v. 3 KJV).

The single game [of the Dan Devine era] that most stands out in people's minds is the victory" over USC in 1977. It wasn't just the win for a team on its way to the national title; it was the clothes.

The Irish wore their traditional blue jerseys during the pre-game warmups for the Oct. 22 game against the fifth-ranked Trojans. Back in the locker room, though, the players discovered green jerseys hanging in each cubicle. They "erupted in surprise and the already sky-high emotions soared even higher."

The Irish "steamed onto the field" and crushed USC 49-19. With the likes of quarterback Joe Montana, 1976 Outland Trophy winner Ross Browner, All-American linebacker Bob Golic, running backs Jerome Heavens and Vagas Ferguson, and All-American tight end Ken MacAfee, Notre Dame was simply loaded in 1977. The green jerseys didn't win the game, but they sure didn't hurt.

The jerseys were such a big deal that day because they had not been worn once during the Ara Parseghian era from 1964-74. Before Parseghian, however, they were worn so often that at one point, the blue jerseys disappeared for seasons at a time.

On Oct. 8, 1921, head coach Knute Rockne used the green jerseys in a game for the first time. Their most dramatic appearance under Rockne came in the 1927 game against the undefeated and defending national champions from Navy. He started his second string, and the Midshipmen quickly scored. Then Rockne had his starting lineup rip off their blue jerseys on the field and change into the green uniforms. Navy didn't score again as Notre Dame rolled 19-6.

The green jerseys reached their zenith during the Frank Leahy era after World War II. The traditional blue jerseys "took a back seat as Leahy started suiting his team up in exclusively green."

Contemporary society proclaims that it's all about the clothes. Buy that new suit or dress, those new shoes, and all the accessories, and you'll be a new person. Like Notre Dame's green jerseys, the changes are only cosmetic, though; under those clothes, you're the same person. Consider Joseph, for instance, prancing about in his pretty new clothes; he was still a spoiled little tattletale whom his brothers detested enough to sell into slavery.

Jesus never taught that we should run around half-naked or wear only second-hand clothes from the local mission. He did warn us, though, against making consumer items such as clothes a priority in our lives. A follower of Christ seeks to emulate Jesus not through material, superficial means such as wearing special clothing like a robe and sandals. Rather, the disciple desires to match Jesus' inner beauty and serenity — whether the clothes the Christian wears are the sables of a king or the rags of a pauper.

It will be remembered forever as 'the Green Jersey Game.'
— Writer Joseph Doyle on the 1977 Southern Cal game

**Where Jesus is concerned,
clothes don't make the person; faith does.**

TURNAROUND

Read Acts 9:1-22.

"All those who heard him were astonished and asked, 'Isn't he the man who raised havoc in Jerusalem among those who call on this name?'" (v. 21)

Luke Harangody was convinced he would be a four-year bench player at Notre Dame. Only a few months later, in an astounding turnaround, he told his head coach not to start him.

From 2006-10, Harangody splattered his name across the Notre Dame record books. As a forward for Mike Brey's men's basketball team, Harangody ended his career as the only Irish player to score more than 2,000 points and pull down 1,000 rebounds. He was the first Irish player to be a three-time first-team All-Big East selection and was named All-America three times.

And yet, some pickup games the summer before his freshman season "were such debacles that he called his father and admitted, "I'm in over my head." Harangody was quite positive he would be nothing but a scrub player at Notre Dame.

The problem was his style of play, honed as he grew up in a household where "physicality [was] central to the family identity." Harangody realized that the "single-minded muscling" that had made him a high-school star wouldn't work in college. So, rather than resign himself to being a scrub, he worked at adding some finesse to his game. The result was a remarkable turnaround.

In Notre Dame's first exhibition game of 2006-07, Harangody

came off the bench and scored 17 points. Within a month, Brey told him he should start. Harangody was horrified. "I didn't see myself in that position" as a freshman, he said. Then Brey uttered a classic line that he probably has never said to another player: "At some point, though, we're going to have to start you."

That point came in January when Brey made the move. Senior guard Colin Falls gave his coach a look that said, "It's about time."

Like Luke Harangody, we often look for some means or some spark to effect a turnaround in our lives. We may not be headed to prison, be bankrupt, or be tormented by an addiction. Maybe we can't find a purpose to our lives and are just drifting.

Still, our situation often seems untenable to us. We sink into gloom and despair. We waste our time, our emotions, and our energy by fretting about how bad things are and how they will never get better. How in the world can we turn things around?

Turn to Jesus; as the old hymn urges, trust and obey him. If it's that simple, then why hesitate? Well, it's also that complicated as Paul discovered when he experienced one of the most dramatic turnarounds in history. To surrender to Jesus is to wind up with a new life, and to wind up with a new life, we have to surrender to Jesus. We have to give up control.

What's to lose? After all, if we're looking for a way to turn our lives around, we're not doing such a good job of running things. What's to gain? A better life here and an eternal life with God.

At least I'm going to get a degree from a great university.
— Luke Harangody to his dad on being a scrub player at Notre Dame

A life in need of turning around
needs Jesus at the wheel.

A GOOD IMPRESSION

Read John 1:1-18.

"In the beginning was the Word, and the Word was with God, and the Word was God. . . . The Word became flesh and made his dwelling among us" (vv. 1, 14).

Women left him their phone numbers, and so many people gathered in front of the door to his dorm room that it scared him off. Yep, that was quite an impression Darius Walker made.

On Sept. 11, 2004, late in the first quarter, Walker entered a college football game for the first time ever. His mom once observed of her son, "He loves the stage." This was one of the biggest stages college football had to offer: the Michigan game. The Wolverines were ranked 8th in the country and were favored; the game was at home and was nationally televised. The freshman desperately wanted to make a good first impression. He did just that.

Walker carried the ball 31 times for 115 yards that day. More impressively, he scored a pair of fourth-quarter touchdowns to propel the Irish to a 28-20 upset.

Then he got a taste of the impression he had made. When he returned to his dorm room a few hours after the game, thirty to forty people were there waiting for him. "I'm like 18 at the time, so I have no idea what's happening," he said. He ran off, taking shelter in a friend's room for a while before trying again.

This time instead of the people, he found a giant white sheet of paper on the floor. Written on it were messages such as, "We're your biggest fans" and "You're our savior." A number of women had left him their phone numbers.

"It was the most ridiculous thing I had ever seen," Walker said, "but it was also the most humbling thing I had ever seen."

Walker went on to make a lasting impression. He turned pro after three seasons, leaving as the school's fourth-leading rusher. He set the school record for most catches by a running back.

That person in the apartment next door. A job search complete with interview. A twenty-year class reunion. The new neighbors. We are constantly about the fraught task of wanting to make an impression on people. We want them to remember us, obviously in a flattering way, which means we perhaps should be circumspect in our personal conduct.

We make that impression, good or bad, generally in two ways. Even with instant communication on the Internet — perhaps especially with the Internet — we primarily influence the opinion others have of us by our words. After that, we can advance to the next level by making an impression with our actions.

God gave us an impression of himself in exactly the same way. In Jesus, God took the unprecedented step of appearing to mortals as one of us, as mere flesh and bone. We now know for all time the sorts of things God does and the sorts of things God says. In Jesus, God put his divine foot forward to make a good impression on each one of us.

It was my induction into the craziness that is Notre Dame football.
— Darius Walker, recalling the hoopla after the '04 Michigan game

Through Jesus' words and actions,
God seeks to impress us with his love.

GOOD TIMES

Read Psalm 30.

"You turned my wailing into dancing; you removed my sackcloth and clothed me with joy" (v. 11).

The seasons of World War II were pretty good times for the Irish, but they were nothing compared to the good times that followed when the war ended.

Many of Notre Dame's stars of 1941 and '42 were far from home fighting in 1943. Six games into the schedule, the Marines called quarterback Angelo Bertelli into active duty. Sophomore John Lujack came on to finish off a national-championship season.

Players in the various military training programs were moved from one college to another. Assistant coaches Joe McArdle, Bob Snyder, and John Druze were in the service. Math professor and baseball coach Jake Kline stepped in to help coach the team.

In 1944, head coach Frank Leahy went into the Navy as military call-ups decimated the team. The only starter left from the 1943 team was guard Pat Filley. It was not a good time to be playing the military academies, and in 1944, Army blasted Notre Dame 59-0, the worst defeat in Irish football history.

Still, the '44 team finished 8-2 and ranked ninth in the nation under assistant coach Ed McKeever. He took a head coaching job after the season, and Hugh Devore took over as interim coach for 1945. He had to piece together a lineup of freshmen and players rejected by the military. The team finished at 7-2-1, again ranked ninth in the nation.

But with the war ended, Leahy, his coaches, and some veteran stars (some from as far back as 1942) returned to campus for the 1946 season. A golden era began. In the four seasons from 1946 through 1949, the Irish went 38 games without a loss and won the national title three times. Lujack and Leon Hart won the Heisman Trophy. Eleven different players were All-Americas.

Here's a basic but distressing fact about the good times in our lives: They don't last. After the great run from 1946-49, Notre Dame went 4-4-1 in 1950.

We may laugh in the sunshine today, but we do so while we symbolically glance over a shoulder. We know that sometime — maybe tomorrow — we will cry in the rain as the good times suddenly come crashing down around us.

Awareness of the certainty that good times don't endure often drives many of us to lose our lives and our souls in a lifestyle devoted to the frenetic pursuit of "fun." This is nothing more, though, than a frantic, pitiable, and doomed effort to outrun the bad times lurking around the corner.

The good times will come and go. Only when we quit chasing the good times and instead seek the good life through Jesus Christ do we discover an eternity in which the good times will never end. Only then will we be forever joyous.

Few freshman in 1946 would have guessed that when they graduated four years later, their football team wouldn't have lost a single game.
— Writer Joseph Doyle on the good times from 1946-49

Let the good times roll — forever and ever
for the followers of Jesus Christ.

AD MAN

Read Mark 1:21-28.

"News about him spread quickly over the whole region"
(v. 28).

Paul Hornung's path to the Heisman Trophy was filled with intrigue, surprise, and adventure." It also lent credence to the old adage that it pays to advertise.

Hornung arrived in South Bend in 1953. His sophomore season was spent as a backup fullback. In 1995, he blossomed as a halfback and safety. Hornung was no scatback; he stood 6'2" and weighed 215 pounds. He was a true triple threat in that he could run, pass, and kick. But as he was rising, Notre Dame was falling.

The 1956 season was an unmitigated disaster for the team, but not for Hornung. He was "personable, dashing, the 'Golden Boy.'" He played in the era before face masks and "always flashed a winning smile, even in the midst of gridiron battle."

In other words, he was a natural for a good publicist to turn into a star. Charlie Callahan was that publicist. After Hornung finished fifth in the Heisman-Trophy voting in 1955, Callahan loaded his weapons for a Hornung Heisman campaign in 1956.

Hornung truly did it all his senior year. He led the team in rushing, passing, scoring, punting, total offense, field-goal kicking, kickoff return average, and minutes played and finished second in tackles. He also finished second nationally in total offense.

All the while, Callahan worked feverishly, undeterred by the awful 2-8 season the team was suffering through. For instance, the week after Michigan thrashed the Irish 47-14, a relatively new publication featured "the photogenic, smiling Hornung" on its cover. It was *Sports Illustrated*.

On Dec. 4, Callahan's ad campaign paid off when he called Hornung to his office, handed him the phone, and ordered him to tell his mom that he had won the Heisman Trophy.

Commercials and advertisements for products, goods, and services inundate us. Watch NASCAR: Decals cover the cars and the drivers' uniforms. Turn on your computer and ads pop up. TV, radio, newspapers, billboards, every square inch of every wall — everyone's one trying to get the word out the best way possible.

Jesus was no different in that he used the most effective and efficient means of advertising he had at his disposal to spread his message of salvation and hope among the masses. That was word of mouth.

In his ministry, Jesus didn't isolate himself; instead, he moved from town to town among the common folks, preaching, teaching, and healing. Those who encountered Jesus then told others about their experience, thus spreading the news about the good news. Almost two millennia later, nothing's really changed. Speaking to someone else about Jesus remains the best way to get the word out, and the best advertisement of all is a changed life.

For decades, wags [said] Charlie Callahan won the 1956 Heisman Trophy, but they merely inscribed Paul Hornung's name on it.
— *UNHD.com*

**The best advertising for Jesus is word of mouth,
telling others what he has done for you.**

STRANGE BUT TRUE

Read Philippians 2:1-11.

"And being found in appearance as a man, he humbled himself and became obedient to death — even death on a cross!" (v. 7)

Much was strange but true about the early days of football at Notre Dame.

Strange but true: Before football, students competed in rowing, wrestling, running, and — of all things — marbles! Then came soccer and baseball and finally football (in 1887).

Strange but true: Notre Dame's first football All-America had no interest in playing football. He was fullback Louis Salmon. As a freshman in 1900, he displayed such extraordinary skills in recreation classes that someone suggested he try out for the football team. He did and moved right into the lineup. From 1900-03, Salmon scored 250 points (though touchdowns counted only five points), a record that stood until Allen Pinkett broke it in 1984.

Strange but true: In a time when folks didn't travel across the country the way they do now, all eleven players appearing in the school's first-ever football game were from different states. None were from Indiana. The first Indiana player, Stephen Fleming of Fort Wayne, didn't show up until the program's third season.

Strange but true: In a game against Michigan in 1888, a Michigan player was designated as the referee because he knew the rules better than anyone else. Not surprisingly, a dispute arose over whether a touchdown should be allowed.

Strange but true: Except for 1890 and 1891 when no team was fielded, the boys played without what was then called a "coacher" from 1887-1903.

Strange but true: In 1889, upset by the injuries suffered in a game against Northwestern, the school president suggested that football be abolished. Center Frank Fehr talked him out of it.

Some things in life are so strange their existence can't really be explained. How else can we account for the sport of curling, tofu, that people go to bars hoping to meet the "right" person, the proliferation of tattoos, and the behavior of teenagers? Isn't it strange that someone would hear the life-changing message of salvation in Jesus Christ and then walk away from it?

And how strange is that plan of salvation that God has for us? Just consider what God did. He could have come roaring down, annihilating everyone whose sinfulness offended him, which, of course, is pretty much all of us. Then he could have brushed off his hands, nodded the divine head, and left a scorched planet in his wake. All in a day's work.

Instead, God came up with a totally novel plan: He would save the world by becoming a human being, letting himself be humiliated, tortured, and killed, thus establishing a kingdom of justice and righteousness that will last forever.

It's a strange way to save the world — but it's true.

It may sound strange, but many champions are made so by setbacks.
— Olympic champion Bob Richards

It's strange but true: God allowed himself
to be killed on a cross to save the world.

SIZE MATTERS

Read Luke 19:1-10.

"[Zacchaeus] wanted to see who Jesus was, but being a short man he could not, because of the crowd. So he ran ahead and climbed a sycamore-fig tree to see him" (vv. 3-4).

Ed Sullivan was just too small to play for Notre Dame. The Irish head coach even told his assistants to stop recruiting him.

Growing up in Pennsylvania, Sullivan dreamed of playing for Notre Dame. Even he admitted, though, that it was just a dream. "I did not believe that I was good enough to go to Notre Dame," he said. He did, however, at least get a look from Notre Dame line coach Bob McBride because of his legendary high school coach.

Sullivan's problem lay in his size. He weighed all of 155 pounds when he graduated from high school in 1954. But a local guy was one of Notre Dame's so-called unpaid scouts; he had a reputation for recommending good players, and he was high on Sullivan.

So one day he loaded Sullivan and three other guys into an old DeSoto and drove to Notre Dame for a game against Southern Cal. They stayed in the dorms, met the coaches, and played some basketball while the coaches watched.

When Sullivan returned home, he didn't hear anything more from the Irish. He had no way of knowing, of course, that head coach Frank Leahy had told McBride, "Stop recruiting Sullivan. He doesn't meet our physical standards." He also didn't know that McBride had said, "Yeah, but he's always where the ball is."

So Sullivan made his plans to attend William & Mary. He had his books and his room and roommate assignments. When he played in the Pennsylvania All-Star Game, though, McBride was there. Sullivan was on his way to South Bend.

He eventually bulked up to 190 pounds. Only 6'0" tall, he was still too small by Irish standards, but as he put it, "I knew I could work harder than anybody else." He worked his way into the lineup at tackle, center, and linebacker for three seasons. As a senior, the player who was too small was a captain of the '57 team.

Bigger is better! Such is one of the most powerful mantras of our time. We expand our football stadiums. We augment our body parts. Hey, make that a large order of fries! Even our church buildings must be bigger to be better. About the only exception to our all-consuming drive for bigness is our waistlines.

But size obviously didn't matter to Jesus. After all, salvation came to the house of an evil tax collector who was so short he had to climb a tree to catch a glimpse of Jesus. Zacchaeus indeed had a big bank account; he was a big man in town even if his own people scorned him. But none of that — including Zacchaeus' height — mattered. Zacchaeus received salvation because of his repentance, which revealed itself in a changed life.

The same is true for us today. What matters is the size of the heart devoted to our Lord.

They were kind of backing away from me because of my size.
— Ed Sullivan on being recruited by Notre Dame

Size matters to Jesus, but only the size
of the heart of the one who would follow Him.

DAY 80

A SECOND CHANCE

Read John 7:53-8:11.

"'Then neither do I condemn you,' Jesus declared. 'Go now and leave your life of sin'" (v. 8:11).

Steve Beuerlein got a second chance. Notre Dame got a historic comeback win.

Beuerlein figured his college playing days had ended when Lou Holtz was named the Irish head coach after the 1985 season. A senior, Beuerlein had been the starter in '85, but he had thrown thirteen interceptions and only three touchdown passes. He also knew Holtz preferred quarterbacks who could run, and that was not Beuerlein's game.

The first time they met, however, Holtz told Beuerlein that he would be the starter. The coach liked the quarterback's leadership. He warned, Beuerlein, though, that he would play only until he threw his sixth interception. Then he would be benched.

Beuerlein had a steady season, good enough to make him a fourth-round pick in the NFL draft that led to a 17-year career in the pros. He had his sixth interception, though, before the final game of the season against Southern Cal. Holtz met with him and said, "I've already given you the benefit of the doubt. . . . If you throw an interception tomorrow, I'm going to take you out."

Sure enough, in the second quarter, Beuerlein threw a pick. As Holtz had promised, he went to the bench. Tears filled his eyes as he sat, disconsolate that his time at Notre Dame would end in such a miserable way.

Suddenly, though, Holtz was in his face. "Are you ready to play some football, son?" "Yes, sir. You will not regret it," the quarterback replied.

Holtz didn't. Given a second chance, Beuerlein led the team to a comeback that is part of Irish lore. With 12 minutes to play, USC led 37-20. Beuerlein threw touchdown passes to Milt Jackson and Braxston Banks and hit tight end Andy Heck for a 2-point conversion. With two seconds left, John Carney kicked a 19-yard field goal for a 38-37 win.

"If I just had a second chance, I know I could make it work out." Ever said that? If only you could go back and tell your dad one last time you love him, take that job you passed up rather than relocate, or replace those angry shouts at your son with gentle encouragement. If only you had a second chance, a mulligan.

As the story of Jesus' encounter with the adulterous woman illustrates, with God you always get a second chance. No matter how many mistakes you make, God will never give up on you. Nothing you can do puts you beyond God's saving power. You always have a second chance because with God your future is not determined by your past or who you used to be. It is determined by your relationship with God through Jesus Christ.

God is ready and willing to give you a second chance — or a third chance or a fourth chance — if you will give him a chance.

Get your butt back out there and go win us the football game.
— Lou Holtz, giving Steve Beuerlein a second chance vs. USC

You get a second chance with God
if you give him a chance.

A SECOND CHANCE 161

GOOD-BYE

Read John 13:31-38.

"My children, I will be with you only a little longer" (v. 33a).

The Irish said good-bye to the long-standing rivalry with Michigan by blowing the Wolverines out of South Bend.

Michigan folks made no bones about how disrespected they felt after they lost to Notre Dame 13-6 in 2012. Their resentment wasn't necessarily about what had happened on the field. Instead, they declared themselves insulted by Irish athletic director Jack Swarbrick's handing his Michigan counterpart a letter declaring cancellation of the series. It was a slap in the face, they said.

The hard feelings continued on into 2013 when the Michigan head coach quipped that Notre Dame was chickening out of the rivalry. Further feathers were ruffled when the "Chicken Dance" blared across Michigan Stadium after the Wolverines' win.

So on Saturday night, Sept. 6, 2014, college football said good-bye to the series that unofficially began in 1887 when the Michigan squad introduced the Irish to this new game sweeping the nation. (See Devotion No. 1.) This farewell wasn't fond at all.

The Irish demolished Michigan 31-0 in the most lopsided Notre Dame victory in the history of the series. The shutout marked the first time since a loss to Iowa in 1984 — a streak covering 365 games — that Michigan had been shut out.

Normally quite level-headed, starting middle linebacker Joe

Schmidt was simply "outdone by the sheer absurdity of the good-bye [the] defense had just delivered the Wolverines." Before the media after the game, he tried to utter the calm, cautious words customary to such gatherings. Finally, he gave up and declared, "Shoot. This is a great feeling right now."

The fans got in on the good-byes, serenading the Wolverines in the closing minutes with "Na Na Hey Hey Kiss Him Goodbye."

You've stood on the curb and watched someone you love drive off, or you've grabbed a last-minute hug before a plane leaves. Maybe it was a child leaving home for the first time or your best friends moving halfway across the country. It's an extended — maybe even permanent — separation, and good-byes hurt.

Jesus felt the pain of parting too. Throughout his brief ministry, Jesus had been surrounded by and had depended upon his friends and confidants, the disciples. About to leave them, he gathered them for a going-away supper and gave them a heads-up about what was about to happen. In the process, he offered them words of comfort. What a wonderful friend he was! Even though he was the one who was about to suffer unimaginable agony, Jesus' concern was for the pain his friends would feel.

But Jesus wasn't just saying good-bye. He was on his mission of providing the way through which none of us would ever have to say good-bye again.

Notre Dame flat-out demoralized the Wolverines in the programs' last meeting.
— *Writer Matt Fortuna on the 31-0 rout in 2014*

**Through Jesus, we will see the day
when we say good-bye to good-byes.**

A HEX ON YOU

Read Jonah 1.

"Tell us, who is responsible for making all this trouble for us? What did you do?" (v. 8a)

To become the most decorated and celebrated female athlete in Notre Dame cross-country history, Molly Seidel had to overcome not only the other runners but mold in her dorm room, a freak bike accident, and a curse.

On Nov. 21, 2015, Seidel, a senior, won the NCAA cross-country championships, finishing five seconds ahead of the runner-up. She thus became Notre Dame's first national champion in cross country in 73 years. (Oliver Hunter won the individual title in 1942; the men won the team title in 1957.)

For most of her time at Notre Dame, though, it seemed she would be yet another victim of the dreaded "Foot Locker Curse." Since 1993, when Foot Locker began sponsoring the high school cross-country championships, no female champion had won an NCAA cross-country title. Seidel won the Foot Locker title in 2011.

Apparently, the curse hung over her with all its fury when she arrived in South Bend. She spent much of her freshman season sick. "I was coughing up blood on the start line at nationals," she recalled. "People in the finishing chute thought I had tuberculosis or something." What she had was mold in her dormitory. The problem was solved with a move to other quarters. Nevertheless, the season "was kind of a nightmare," she said.

FIGHTING IRISH

Next came what Seidel called "a comedy of errors for two years" that featured a pair of stress fractures. But when Matt Sparks arrived in August 2014 as Notre Dame's distance specialist and assistant track coach, he changed the way Seidel trained. In the spring of 2015, she won the 10,000-meter outdoor championship.

But the curse seemed to rear up again the week of the NCAA run when Seidel had an accident on her bike and "busted up" her knee. It didn't matter; she still won.

As Molly Seidel's championship run in 2015 illustrates, curses, hexes, jinxes, and the like really belong to the domain of superstitious balderdash. Some people do feel, however, that they exist under a dark and rainy cloud. Nothing goes right; all their dreams collapse around them; they seem to constantly bring about misery on themselves and the ones around them.

Why? Is it really a hex, a jinx? Nonsense. The Bible provides us an excellent example in Jonah. The sailors on the boat with the reluctant prophet believed him to be a hex and the source of their bad luck. Jonah's life was a mess, but it had nothing to do with any jinx. His life was in shambles because he was disobeying God.

Take a careful look at people you know whose lives are a big mess, including some who profess to believe in God. The key to life lies not in belief alone; the responsibility of the believer is to obey God. Problems never have their root in hexes and curses; all too often their source is disobedience.

I've been hearing about that stupid curse for years.
— Molly Seidel on the 'Foot Locker Curse'

**Hexes and curses don't cause us trouble,
but disobedience to God sure does.**

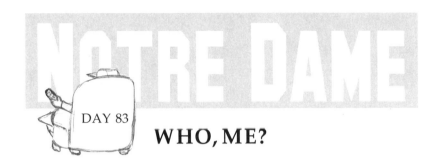

DAY 83

WHO, ME?

Read Judges 6:11-23.

*"'But Lord,' Gideon asked, 'how can I save Israel? My
clan is the weakest in Manasseh, and I am the least in my
family'" (v. 15).*

Terry Hanratty couldn't believe that head coach Ara Parseghian
had called his number. As it turned out, he hadn't, and the play
was a disaster in more ways than one.

As a sophomore in 1966, Hanratty quarterbacked the Irish to a
9-0-1 record and the national championship. After his first-ever
game, a 26-14 defeat of Purdue, he and sophomore receiver Jim
Seymour were on the cover of *Time*. His mother was relatively
unimpressed. When Hanratty called her after the game, all she
could talk about was Purdue quarterback Bob Griese and how her
son should try to be like him.

Hanratty and Seymour often practiced in an old field house. To
complete a pass of 40 yards or longer, he had to arc it over several
rafters. The lighting was terrible. "If you could catch the ball in
there, you could catch it anywhere," Hanratty said.

The 10-10 tie with Michigan State in 1966 is still remembered as
one of the biggest games in college football history. It was during
the third offensive series of the game that Hanratty had his disastrous "Who, Me?" moment.

The offense was driving when a play came in from the sideline:
a quarterback draw. The call puzzled Hanratty because he hadn't

practiced it in a while. Nevertheless, he ran it. He took three steps back and didn't even get started before he was swamped.

When Hanratty got to his feet, his left shoulder "felt a little weird." The next play was a pass, but as soon as Hanratty raised his arm to throw, he knew his shoulder was separated

Parseghian was waiting for him when he came off the field. The rather perturbed coach wanted to know why in the world Hanratty had run a draw. You sent it in, was the reply. "No," the coach said. "That was supposed to be a halfback draw!"

You probably know exactly how Terry Hanratty felt; you've experienced that moment of unwelcome surprise with its sinking "who, me?" feeling. How about that time the teacher called on you when you hadn't done a lick of homework? What about testifying in court? Or having to deliver bad news to the family? You've had the wide-eyed look and the turmoil in your midsection when you were suddenly singled out and found yourself in a situation you neither sought nor were prepared for.

You may feel exactly as Gideon did about being called to serve God in some way, quailing at the very notion of being audacious enough to teach Sunday school, coordinate a high school prayer club, or lead a small group study. Who, me? Hey, who's worthy enough to do anything like that?

The truth is that nobody is — but that doesn't seem to matter to God. And it's his opinion, not yours, that counts.

I couldn't figure out why Ara would call for [a quarterback draw].
— Terry Hanratty on the 'Who, me?' play vs. Michigan State

**You're right in that no one is worthy to serve God,
but the problem is that doesn't matter to God.**

STORM WARNING

Read Luke 12:4-10.

"Whoever acknowledges me before men, the Son of Man will also acknowledge him before the angels of God. But he who disowns me before men will be disowned before the angels of God" (vv. 8-9).

Pete Chryplewicz had been warned. As a result, Notre Dame kept one of its best tight ends ever.

In 1992, Chryplewicz was a struggling freshman when senior tight end Irv Smith pulled him aside and issued his warning. The veteran told the rookie that head coach Lou Holtz would test him. He said at some point Holtz would tell Chryplewicz to get off his team or his field or to transfer. "Go get some water, then come right back in the huddle the next play," Smith advised.

In 1993, Chryplewicz was set to start at tight end for the 7-0 Irish against USC (a 31-13 win). The lineman opposite him would be an All-America and a first-round pick in the 1994 draft.

"It was a long, hard week for me," Chryplewicz recalled. Holtz rotated four players against him with instructions to hit him over and over again. Thursday, Chryplewicz received a message that Holtz wanted to see him. He figured the head man would offer him congratulations for making it through the tough week.

Instead, Holtz told him he would be a great player, but "you're not cut out for Notre Dame." He told Chryplewicz not to bother coming to practice that day and that he would write a letter of recommendation to whatever school he wanted to play for. Then the coach went to work, effectively dismissing Chryplewicz.

The stunned player left the office before he recalled the warning Smith had given him the season before. He turned around, went back into the office, and told his head coach, "I'm staying. I'm not transferring. I'm going to start for you this Saturday."

Chryplewicz stayed and started. In 1996, he became the first tight end since Mark Bavaro in 1984 to lead the Irish in receptions.

Our household alarm system warns us of an intruder. A tornado warning makes us wary. Our nation has a whole system devoted to different levels of warning about the possibility of a terrorist attack. At railroad crossings, signals with their flashing lights and clanging bells warn us of an approaching train.

Individually, we are ever on the alert for the warning signs of health problems such as cancer, heart attack, and stroke. Relationship specialists speak of the warning signs of a distressed marriage or a bad relationship.

We heed or ignore these various warnings in direct relation to the sense of urgency they carry for us. No warning, however, should be as urgent for all of us as the one Jesus Christ issued. In his matter-of-fact way, Jesus warned us: Claim him during our life and be claimed as God's own in Heaven; reject him and be banned from Heaven.

We've been warned.

I was just floored! My heart dropped, my stomach ached.
—Pete Chryplewicz before he remembered Irv Smith's warning

Jesus warned us that if we reject him
here on Earth, he will reject us in Heaven.

GOD'S HOUSE

Read 2 Samuel 7:1-7.

"I have not dwelt in a house from the day I brought the Israelites up out of Egypt to this day. I have been moving from place to place with a tent as my dwelling" (v. 6).

There has never been — nor will there ever be — another building on the Notre Dame campus quite like The Fieldhouse.

The Old Fieldhouse was built in 1898 and promptly burned down. Father Andrew Morrissey, the university president, rebuilt it quickly, using steel and concrete to render it fireproof.

The building had a clay floor, which had to be watered down and rolled before basketball games. Proceeds from the 1925 Rose Bowl were spent on a hardwood floor. Track-and-field events and indoor baseball and football practices were also held there.

Beginning on Friday evenings in the 1920s, the Fieldhouse hosted pep rallies that turned the place into "a pressurized capsule of cacophony." The gatherings were "so boisterous that the sound carried for miles beyond the farms that ringed campus." The students jammed the old building that had the "color scheme of a dungeon" and stood shoulder to shoulder with one goal in mind: to outyell the other guys. They climbed on each other and created human pyramids. One student described the scene as "kind of like going to the circus without the elephants."

One pep rally in particular became legendary. The Irish had been tied by Iowa the Saturday before, the only blemish in a

9-0-1 season. The students were already going wild when a team captain took over the microphone. He had dropped a touchdown pass in the end zone in the game and tried to speak, but broke down and cried instead. The students gave him a standing ovation that lasted for thirty-eight minutes. "I know. I timed it," said a freshman who was there — a guy named Paul Hornung.

The last basketball game was played there in 1968, and a real homefield advantage was gone. The final record was 474-91.

Buildings such as The Old Fieldhouse, which was razed in 1983, play a pivotal roles in our lives, and we often become sentimentally attached to them. A favorite restaurant. A football stadium or basketball gymnasium. The house you grew up in.

But what about a church? How important is that particular facility to you? Is it just the place where you were married? Where you were baptized? Is it nothing more than a house of memories or a place you visit out of habit to placate the spouse?

Or is it the place where you regularly go to meet God? After all, a church building is a place built expressly for God. It's God house. Long ago, the only place God could visit his people was in a lousy tent. Nowadays, churches serve as the site where God's people meet both to worship and to encounter him.

In a church alive with a true love of God, he is always there. Whether you find him or not depends on how hard you look. And whether you're searching for him with your heart.

[Father Morrissey] had no idea that this gray, castellated edifice would someday become the spiritual center of Notre Dame athletics.
— Writer Jim Dent on the Old Fieldhouse

When you visit God in his house, do you find him?

DAY 86

THE DIGGINS TEN

Read Exodus 20:1-17.

"God spoke all these words: 'I am the Lord your God . . . .
You shall have no other gods before me'" (vv. 1, 3).

I don't know that we'll ever have another player like her." So spoke Irish head coach Muffet McGraw about Skylar Diggins.

From 2009-2013, Diggins rewrote the Notre Dame record book. She set career records for points, steals, free throws made, free throws attempted, games started, minutes played, double-figure scoring games, and triple-doubles. She was twice named the best point guard in the country and was a two-time All-America.

Much is known about her through the media, but below is a list of ten things you may not know about the person generally considered Notre Dame's greatest women's basketball player.

1) McGraw offered Diggins a scholarship when she was in the eighth grade, the only time she has ever done anything like that.

2) Diggins didn't arrive at Notre Dame as a point guard. McGraw's instructions to her for her new position were basic: When you're open, shoot it; when you're not, give it up.

3) Diggins is a self-proclaimed girly girl. Before every game, she had her eyebrows and nails done and often changed her hairstyle at halftime depending on how she was playing.

4) Among the rules in her house growing up were a permanent ban on the word "can't" and an 11 p.m. curfew.

5) She came close to signing with Stanford at the last minute.

6) At Notre Dame, her Twitter account had more than 120,000 followers, more than any other college player, male or female.

7) In high school, when Diggins had a date, her mom would write down the license-plate number of the boy's car and demand a cellphone number.

8) She was an AAU star by the time she was nine.

9) At Notre Dame, she started all but one game. She gave up her starting spot on Feb. 26, 2011, to allow walk-on Mary Forr to start on Senior Day.

10) She was in the 2014 *Sports Illustrated* swimsuit edition.

Like this list about Skylar Diggins, we employ lists in our life. We are advised not to go to the grocery store without a list, and we often set out on a list of errands. Our lists help us remember.

God also made a list of things he wants us to remember. We have come to call God's list The Ten Commandments. Just as our lists remind to do something, so does God's list remind us of how we to act in our dealings with other people and with him.

A life dedicated to Jesus is a life devoted to relationships, and God's list emphasizes that the social life and the spiritual life of the faithful cannot be sundered. God's relationship to us is one of unceasing, unqualified love, and we are to mirror that divine love in our relationships with others. In case we forget, we have a list.

Society today treats the Ten Commandments as if they were the ten suggestions. Never compromise on right or wrong.
— Former college baseball coach Gordie Gillespie

**God's top ten list is a set of instructions
on how you are to conduct yourself
with other people and with him.**

DAY 87

ZINGERS

Read Luke 20:9-19.

"The teachers of the law and the chief priests looked for a way to arrest him . . . because they knew he had spoken . . . against them" (v. 19).

Some unknown persons on the LSU football team made a big mistake before their match-up with Notre Dame: They called the Irish players fat slobs.

All week long before the game of Nov. 21, 1970, the Irish players passed by their message board, which bore a newspaper clipping with a particularly nasty insult from the Tigers. It read, "Notre Dame: They're fat slobs."

All-American receiver Tom Gatewood didn't like it one bit. He set a school record in 1970 with 77 receptions and was inducted into the College Football Hall of Fame in 2015. He called the insult, "humiliating. I've never been vengeful for anything. Man, this week I am."

Defensive end Walt Patulski didn't like it either. He would earn All-American honors and win the Lombardi Award as the nation's best lineman in 1971. "If they want to make it a slugfest," he said, "I'd like that. They'll see I'm not a fat slob."

As it turned out, the game *was* a slugfest, a magnificent one. One writer called it "a game of Ping Pong played with a football," "as glorious a defensive game as one could hope to see."

Neither the undefeated Irish nor the 7-1 Tigers gave up much of anything, especially points. When Jim Yoder punted LSU into a hole inside its 1-yard line with 6:50 left to play, someone in the press box asked, "Would you believe 2-nothin'?" That's because the game was scoreless.

The defense held and Clarence Ellis returned the punt to the 36. After a penalty, Scott Hempel kicked a field goal from 24 yards out with 2:54 left. With nary a fat slob in this bitterly contested game, Notre Dame won 3-0.

There's nothing like a good insult to rile us up. We take a nasty zinger just as the 1970 Irish did: personally.

Few people throughout history can match Jesus, of all people, for delivering a well-placed zinger, and few insults throughout history can match the one he tossed at the religious authorities in Luke 20. Jesus' remarks were so accurate and so severe that the targets of his insult responded by seeking to have him arrested.

Using a vineyard as the centerpiece of an extensive allegory, Jesus insulted the priests and their lackeys by declaring that they had insulted God in rejecting his rule over them. They had sought to own God's kingdom for themselves.

They were truly just a bunch of hypocrites. But before we get too smug, we need to take a good look around. Little has changed. We still seek to live our lives on our terms, not God's. The world is in such a mess because we want to run God's vineyard, instead of surrendering to him. Jesus delivered that insult right at us.

I've never been called a slob in my life.
— *Tom Gatewood before the 1970 LSU game*

**In insulting the priests for rebelling against God,
Jesus delivered a zinger right at us.**

OPPORTUNITY KNOCKS

Read Colossians 4:2-6.

"[M]ake the most of every opportunity" (v. 5b).

DeShone Kizer had the opportunity of a lifetime, and he blew it big time.

On May 22, 2013, Ohio State and Notre Dame sent their top assistants to Toledo "to watch a precocious high-school junior go through a half-hour throwing session." Kizer was that player. He already had a number of offers in his pocket, but the Buckeyes and the Irish still needed convincing.

Wanting desperately to impress the two coaches, Kizer put on a show. It was the wrong kind, though. "It looked like the Wild West," said Notre Dame's offensive coordinator, Chuck Martin. "There were balls gusting everywhere. One hitch [pass] bounced like halfway there. It was bad."

Kizer realized he had dropped the ball with his great opportunity. He told his college counselor, "I was terrible. The worst I've thrown in years." He said the Notre Dame coach "just left, and I kind of just X-ed them out." His counselor replied, "If God wants you to be at Notre Dame, you're going to be at Notre Dame. There is nothing one day will change."

She was dead on. Ohio State never offered Kizer a scholarship, but the Irish coaches had not lost the faith. Martin wrote the day off as an anomaly. When Kizer called the coach and offered to throw for him again, Martin declined. "I'm good," he said. Martin later told Kizer's coach Notre Dame was going to offer Kizer a scholarship. Days later, he committed.

In 2015, Kizer proved to be "an answered prayer" for the Irish. When Malik Zaire suffered a broken leg in the second game, Kizer was suddenly the starting quarterback. He grew into a star, throwing for twenty-one touchdowns, rushing for ten more, and guiding the Irish to a ten-win season and a Fiesta-Bowl berth.

As he worked out that May morning in 2013, DeShone Kizer understood that opportunities usually come around only once. Miss the chance and it's gone forever. The house you wanted that came on the market; that chance for promotion that opened up, the accidental meeting with that person you've been attracted to at a distance; that job interview — if the opportunity comes, you have to grab it right now or you may well miss it.

This doesn't hold true in our faith life, however. Salvation through Jesus Christ is not a one-and-done deal. As long as we live, every day and every minute of our life, the opportunity to turn to Jesus is always with us. We have unlimited access to the saving grace of our Lord and Savior.

As with any opportunity, though, we must avail ourselves of it. That is, salvation is ours for the taking but we must take it. The inherent tragedy of an unsaved life thus is not that the opportunity for salvation was withdrawn or unavailable, but that it was squandered.

You could tell he was really pressing, and we've all seen that.
— Notre Dame coach Chuck Martin on DeShone Kizer's workout

We have the opportunity for salvation through Jesus Christ at any time.

DAY 89

CONFIDENCE MEN

Read Micah 7:1-7.

"As for me, I will look to the Lord, I will wait for the God of my salvation" (v. 7 NRSV).

Facing a game about which his players could have no reason for any confidence, Irish head coach Digger Phelps came up with a remarkable ploy that gave them some. It helped the team pull off the most memorable win in Notre Dame men's basketball history.

On Jan. 19, 1974, the Irish were big underdogs against UCLA. They weren't bad; in fact, they were 9-0. But they were up against a UCLA squad that featured eight future NBA players, including Bill Walton. The Bruins had won 88 straight games, the longest streak ever, and seven national titles in a row.

Not surprisingly, as game-day neared, Phelps was searching for some way he could instill some confidence into his team. The Wednesday before the game, he found it. At the end of practice, he called his team together and gave them some specific instructions — on how to go about cutting down the nets! He then told them to practice it. As Phelps recalled it, "Some of [the players] looked at me like I was crazy, but they did it."

With 3:32 left, it looked as though the team had played confidently but not well enough as UCLA led 70-59. What happened after that was pure Irish magic. The rest of the game, Notre Dame forced UCLA into "four puerile turnovers" and outscored the Bruins 12-0. They "were swept away on a tide of panic as their elegant play turned crude," wrote *SI's* Barry McDermott.

The final blow came with 29 seconds left. The Irish trailed 70-69. Gary Brokaw drove to the top of the key, spotted junior guard Dwight Clay open in the right corner, and got the ball to him. Clay confidently nailed it for the 71-70 lead that held up.

At game's end, the students rushed the court, thus keeping the players from cutting the nets as they had so carefully practiced it. "It was the only thing we messed up the whole day," Phelps said.

As do the Irish, you need confidence in all areas of your life. You're confident the company you work for will pay you on time. You turn the ignition confident your car will start. When you flip a switch, you expect the light to come on.

Confidence in other people and in things is often misplaced, though. Companies go broke; car batteries die; light bulbs burn out. Even the people you love the most sometimes let you down.

So where can you place your trust with absolute confidence you won't be betrayed? In the promises of God.

Such confidence is easy, of course, when everything's going your way, but what about when you cry as Micah did, "What misery is mine!" As Micah declares, that's when your confidence in God must be its strongest. That's when you wait for the Lord confident that God will not fail you, that he will never let you down.

You couldn't underestimate the importance of confidence when you were playing UCLA.

— *Digger Phelps*

People, things, and organizations will let you down; only God can be trusted confidently.

DAY 90

PROBLEMS, PROBLEMS

Read James 1:2-12.

"Blessed is the man who perseveres under trial, because when he has stood the test, he will receive the crown of life that God has promised to those who love him" (v. 12).

Notre Dame's new head football coach discovered he had several problems on his hands, not the least of which was a quarterback who'd rather be playing tennis.

Dan Devine coached the Irish from 1975-80. His 1977 team went 11-1 and won the national title by beating top-ranked Texas 38-10 in the Cotton Bow. The squad featured All-Americans Ken MacAfee, Ross Browner, Luther Bradley, and Bob Golic.

That success was down the road when Devine arrived in 1975 and had some problems on his hands. His offense was missing ten starters. His young charges — desperately in need of practice — kept wandering in late from class or leaving early to attend class.

The media were frothing over the suspension of some players over the summer. One player had his scholarship terminated after a marijuana bust. Safety Tim Simon was fencing with bamboo sticks and had one break off in his eye. A tight end had to quit because of a chronic nerve injury. The first week of practice, starting quarterback Frank Allocco separated his shoulder.

That left the team in the hands of junior Rick Slager, which was another problem. He had come to Notre Dame in the first place to play tennis. In fact, he had played more tennis (no. 1 in varsity singles) than he had football (18 minutes total). He was a pre-med student who didn't resemble a typical quarterback. He stood 5'11" with a physique his buddy, halfback Mark McLane, described as "chunky." Center Steve Quehl, another pal, just called him "fat."

Despite all those problems, the Irish did all right. They went 8-3 in '75 and 9-3 in '76 with Slager over center. The '76 team finished in the top 20 and laid the foundation for the title of '77.

Problems are such a ubiquitous feature of our lives that a whole day — all twenty-four hours — without a single problem ranks up there with a government without taxes, a Notre Dame sports program that never, ever loses, and entertaining, wholesome TV programs. We just can't even imagine it.

But that's life. Even Jesus had his share of problems, especially with his twelve-man staff. Jesus could have easily removed all problems from his daily walk, but what good would that have done us? Our goal is to become like Jesus, and we could never fashion ourselves after a man who didn't encounter job stress, criticism, loneliness, temptation, frustration, and discouragement.

Instead, Jesus showed us that when — not if — problems come, a person of faith uses them to get better rather than letting the problems use him to get bitter. We learn God-filled perseverance and patience as we develop and deepen our faith and our trust in God. Problems will pass; eternity will not.

The pressure doesn't scare me.
— Dan Devine on a problem that came with the Notre Dame job

**The problem with problems is that we often
let them use us and become bitter rather than
using them to become better.**

HURRY UP AND WAIT

Read Acts 1:1-14.

"Do not leave Jerusalem, but wait for the gift my Father promised, which you have heard me speak about" (v. 4).

The game was over; Notre Dame had won. Or maybe not. The Irish faithful could only wait — and wait and wait — to find out.

The Notre Dame-Stanford game of 2012 was an exciting thriller with a legendary goal-line stand and an unusual and controversial finish. On Oct. 13, the undefeated and 7th-ranked Irish hosted the once-defeated No. 17 Cardinal. Kyle Brindza's 22-yard field goal with 20 seconds left in regulation tied the score at 13-13 and sent the game into overtime.

In the extra period, backup quarterback Tommy Rees found Theo Riddick for 16 yards on third-and-eight. That set up a 7-yard touchdown toss to TJ Jones.

The 20-13 score was placed in serious jeopardy, however. The Cardinal responded to the Notre Dame score by driving to a first down at the Irish 4-yard line. The Notre Dame defense had not given up a rushing touchdown all season, and they were in no mood to start now. Three plays left Stanford at the 1.

Cornerback Bennett Jackson said "Everybody looked at each other. I don't think one person said one word. We understood what we needed to do, what had to be done." At the snap, Jackson blitzed, grabbed the Stanford back by the legs, and held on until linebacker Carlo Calabrese showed up to finish him off.

FIGHTING IRISH

The refs ruled the Cardinal back had been stopped short of the goal line. Game over. A wild celebration began that almost immediately ended when the announcement came that the play was under review. Everyone waited anxiously for what seemed like the longest 3:16 in Irish history.

The decision finally came: Despite his protests, the Stanford back had not scored. The play stood as called; the wait was over.

You rush to your doctor's appointment and wind up sitting in the appropriately named waiting room for an hour. You wait in the concessions line at a Notre Dame game. You're put on hold when you call a tragically misnamed "customer service" center. All of that waiting is time in which we seem to do nothing but feel the precious minutes of our life ticking away.

Sometimes we even wait for God. We have needs, and in our desperation, we call upon the Lord. We are then disappointed if we don't get an immediate answer to our prayers.

But Jesus' last command to his disciples was to wait. Moreover, the entire of our Christian life is spent in an attitude of waiting for Jesus' return. While we wait for God, we hold steadfast to his promises, and we continue our ministry; we remain in communion with him through prayer and devotion.

In other words, we don't just wait; we grow stronger in our faith. Waiting for God is never time lost.

I was still celebrating. I was gonna celebrate until that call was made.
— Bennett Jackson on what he did while everyone waited

Since God acts on his time and not ours,
we often must wait for him,
using the time to strengthen our faith.

NOW HEAR THIS

Read Luke 1:26-38.

"God sent the angel Gabriel . . . to a virgin. . . . The angel said to her, "You will . . . give birth to a son, and you are to give him the name Jesus" (vv. 26, 27, 30, 31).

In three remarkable nights, Notre Dame's men's basketball team boldly announced that the program had arrived in the ACC.

As expected, the Irish took their licks in 2013-14, their first season in the Atlantic Coast Conference, arguably college basketball's toughest league. They went 6-12 in ACC play and stumbled to the program's first losing season since 1988-89.

In 2014-15, however, the Irish put the program back on its feet. They went 14-4 in league play to finish third, won 26 games, and ended the season ranked No. 11 in the country. But the new kids on the block still had to prove themselves.

The real proving ground was the ACC Tournament. To win it, the Irish had to get by Miami and then beat league bluebloods Duke and North Carolina on successive nights.

The Hurricanes went down 70-63 and then Duke fell 71-64. That put the rookies from South Bend in the tournament finals against North Carolina, which was making its 33rd title-game appearance.

Sure enough, UNC led by nine with 9:58 to go. But then came a run of what head coach Mike Brey called "beautiful basketball" that was like "a lightning strike." Over the next seven minutes, the Irish made four 3-pointers, stole the ball five times, and went up by 12 points. They won 90-82.

Cutting down the nets as league champions provided the exclamation point to the announcement that the Irish had arrived in the ACC.

As we understand it today, an announcement is a declaration that is publicly distributed. Interestingly, the greatest — and certainly the most unexpected — announcement in history was delivered to only one person.

What Gabriel announced to a young peasant girl was nothing less than the unfolding of God's grand design for the salvation of sin-ridden humanity. The fancy phrase for it all is the annunciation of the incarnation of Jesus Christ. In other words, Gabriel told Mary she would give birth to Jesus, the savior of the world; God was about to enter human life.

When we receive a wedding or graduation announcement, or a couple announces they are expecting a child, we are free to respond to that news pretty much how we wish. We can be joyful, excited, or indifferent.

That freedom is likewise available for us with Gabriel's great announcement. In Mary's response to this life-changing and confusing news, we see the example of how we are to react to the claims God makes on our lives: with total obedience, no matter the personal cost.

For one weekend, Notre Dame finalized its arrival in the ACC.
— Writer Mike Monaco on the 2015 ACC Tournament

Centuries after it was made, God's grand announcement still demands a response from us.

TIME FOR A CHANGE

Read Romans 6:1-14.

"Just as Christ was raised from the dead through the glory of the Father, we too may live a new life" (v. 4).

Frank Leahy once instituted a change so radical that the repercussions from it landed him in the hospital.

When Irish head coach Elmer Layden resigned following the 1940 season, Leahy left Boston College to take his dream job in South Bend. In his first season, the Irish went 8-0-1 and finished third in the country. The team was led by Angelo Bertelli, who became Notre Dame's first 1,000-yard passer in a season.

Football was changing, though, with the new T formation suddenly the rage. Leahy realized that the formation was perfect for Bertelli's passing ability. He also appreciated the enormity of what the change to the T would entail: dumping the old box formation used so successfully by Irish icon Knute Rockne.

Leahy sought and received permission from the school's executive vice president to make the radical change. "We started almost as soon as the '41 season was over," Bertelli said about installing the new scheme. "We practiced hours and hours."

It didn't come easy. Bertelli was overwhelmed by calling the plays and the signals and then executing. The '42 season started with a 7-7 tie against Wisconsin and a 13-6 loss to Georgia Tech.

The head coach "was eviscerated by Notre Dame alumni for daring to repair what wasn't broken." The Thursday before the

FIGHTING IRISH

third game, Leahy collapsed at his desk and was hospitalized. He missed the game, but he had already made a big change. He had assigned signal calling to guard Harry Wright and halfback Pete Ashbaugh. That freed Bertelli up to concentrate on passing.

The change worked. The team finished 7-2-2, setting the stage for the 1943 national title run in which the unstoppable offense averaged 43.5 points per game. Bertelli won the Heisman Trophy. The change also worked for other Notre Dame quarterbacks. Under Leahy's tutelage, John Lujack, Bob Williams, and Ralph Guglielmi had Hall-of-Fame careers. Lujack won the Heisman.

Anyone who asserts no change is needed in his or her life just isn't paying attention. Every life has doubt, worry, fear, failure, frustration, unfulfilled dreams, and unsuccessful relationships in some combination. The memory and consequences of our past often haunt and trouble us.

Simply recognizing the need for change in our lives, though, doesn't mean the changes that will bring about hope, joy, peace, and fulfillment will occur. We need some power greater than ourselves or we wouldn't be where we are.

So where can we turn to? Where lies the hope for a changed life? It lies in an encounter with the Lord of all Hope: Jesus Christ. For a life turned over to Jesus, change is inevitable. With Jesus in charge, the old self with its painful and destructive ways of thinking, feeling, loving, and living is transformed.

A changed life is always only a talk with Jesus away.

It was all brand new to us.
      — Angelo Bertelli on the change to the T formation

In Jesus lie the hope and the power to change lives.

HERO WORSHIP

Read 1 Samuel 16:1-13.

"Do not consider his appearance or his height, for . . . the Lord does not look at the things man looks at. . . . The Lord looks at the heart" (v. 7).

Against mighty Michigan in the 1988 season opener, the unlikeliest folk hero in Notre Dame football history emerged.

The '88 team "is considered to be one of the best undefeated teams in the history of college football." They went 12-0, beating the Nos. 1, 2, and 3 teams at the time they played them. In the opener on Sept. 10, though, the Irish were underdogs to the 9th-ranked Wolverines. They would need somebody to step up. That somebody turned out to be Reggie Ho.

With plans of becoming a doctor, Ho spent most of his freshman season in the library, which led to a whole bunch of A's. He decided he wanted to be more than, as he put it, "a nerd who studies too much." A soccer player at his high school in Honolulu, Ho decided to try out for Lou Holtz's football team.

He made the team in the spring of '87 and served as Ted Gradel's backup that season. He kicked one extra point in the 56-13 blowout of Navy. As the '88 season began, Holtz named him the team's short-range kicker. Billy Hackett would handle kickoffs and field goals longer than 40 yards.

Nothing about Ho was typical. He was 5'5" tall and weighed 135 pounds, by far the team's smallest player. TV announcer Pat

Haden said he had to get his jersey in the bookstore. Before each kick, Ho would line up behind holder Pete Graham, "swing both arms to his right [and] wiggle his fingers" before driving the ball. Haden called it "this voodoo or this kung fu routine of his." Even Ho's brother, Tim, said it looked silly.

But it worked. Ho was 3-for-3 on field goals when he trotted onto the field for a 26-yard try with 1:19 left. His true kick beat Michigan 19-17, and Notre Dame had a brand new folk hero.

A hero is commonly thought of as someone who performs brave and dangerous feats that save or protect someone's life or someone who pulls off remarkable athletic feats under pressure as Reggie Ho did. You figure that excludes you.

But ask your son about that when you show him how to bait a hook or throw a football, or your daughter when you show up for her honors night at school. Look into the eyes of those Little Leaguers you help coach.

Ask God about heroism when you're steady in your faith. For God, a hero is a person with the heart of a servant. And if a hero is a servant who acts to save other's lives, then the greatest hero of all is Jesus Christ.

God seeks heroes today, those who will proclaim the name of their hero — Jesus — proudly and boldly, no matter how others may scoff or ridicule. God knows true heroes when he sees them — by what's in their hearts.

Going 4-for-4 against Michigan, Ho kind of became a folk hero, really.
— Lou Somogyi of Blue & Gold Illustrated

God's heroes are those who remain steady
in their faith while serving others.

THE END

Read Revelation 22:8-17.

"I am the Alpha and the Omega, the First and the Last, the Beginning and the End" (v. 13).

The end of an era had arrived, and the Irish players were determined it would not go out with a loss.

After the 14-6 win over Navy on Nov 2, 1974, Ara Parseghian decided that the season would be his last as Notre Dame's head coach. The Ara Era was a great one for the school. It was an 11-year run that yielded two national championships, nine top-ten finishes, and an overall record of 95-17-4.

Only 51, Parseghian "was just worn out" after twenty-four straight seasons as a head coach. He was taking sleeping pills and blood pressure medicine. When the season ended with a loss to Southern Cal that dropped the team to 9-2, he briefly considered not resigning before making his decision public.

Parseghian's last game at Notre Dame was the 1975 Orange Bowl against undefeated and top-ranked Alabama, not a first choice for hopes of ending a storied career with a win. The head coach sought to deflect attention from himself by telling his team "they didn't owe me anything, but [they] owed it to themselves to play a great game." They did.

Despite being weakened by the flu, fullback Wayne Bullock, the team's leading rusher, and halfback Mark McLane scored first-half touchdowns for a 13-3 Irish lead. The Tide rallied to cut the lead to 13-11 with 3:13 left and then got the ball back with under two minutes to play.

Needing only a field goal to win it, Alabama completed two passes to move downfield. With 1:08 left, though, cornerback Reggie Barnett hauled in an interception at the Irish 34. "It was the biggest play I ever made," Barnett said.

The players carried their victorious head coach off the field on their shoulders as he pumped his fist into the air. The Era of Ara had ended just as it had begun: with a win.

Ara Parseghian's career at Notre Dame is another example of one of life's basic truths: Everything ends. Even the stars have a life cycle, though admittedly it's rather lengthy. Erosion eventually will wear a boulder to a pebble. Life itself is temporary; all living things have a beginning and an end.

Within the framework of our own lifetimes, we experience endings. Loved ones, friends, and pets die; relationships fracture; jobs dry up; our health, clothes, lawn mowers, TV sets, cars — they all wear out. Even this world as we know it will end.

But one of the greatest ironies of God's gift of life is that not even death is immune from the great truth of creation that all things must end. That's because through Jesus' life, death, and resurrection, God himself acted to end any power death once had over life. In other words, because of Jesus, the end of life has ended. Eternity is ours for the claiming.

That was a much more pleasant way of leaving the game.
— Ara Parseghian on ending his career with a win

**Everything ends; thanks to Jesus Christ,
so does death.**

THE END   191

NOTES
(by Devotion Day Number)

1   Wanting to learn the . . . as was a cheerleader.: Joseph Doyle, *Fighting Irish: A Century of Notre Dame Football* (Charlottesville, Va.: Howell Press, 1987), p. 33.

1   The visitors took an hour . . . the Michigan players departed.": William Gildea and Christopher Jennison, *The Fighting Irish: Notre Dame Football Through the Years* (Englewood Cliffs, N.J.: Prentice-Hall, Inc., 1976), p. 20.

1   The game was interesting, and . . . a series of these contests.: Gildea and Jennison, p. 20.

2   Concerned about his grades, . . . on the junior varsity.: Andy Staples, "For Notre Dame's Tuitt, Path to BCS Began on Georgia Road," *SI.com*, Jan. 2, 2013, http://sportsillustrated.cnn.com/college-football/news/20130102/stephen-tuitt-notre-dame.

2   He took the long way.: Staples, "For Notre Dame's Tuitt, Path to BCS Began on Georgia Road."

3   He redesigned his team's . . . on football game days.: Digger Phelps with Tim Bourret, *Digger Phelps's Tales from the Notre Dame Hardwood* (Champaign, Ill.: Sports Publishing L.L.C., 2004), p. 4.

3   "I loved the essence . . . Notre Dame men's basketball coach.: Tim Bourret, "Digger Phelps and Notre Dame: A Dream Realized," *UND.COM*, Jan. 18, 2014, http://www.und.com/sports/m-baskbl/spec-rel/011814aaa.html.

3   When the new head went . . . in the press guide that fall.: Phelps with Bourret, p. 12.

3   It does seem crazy . . . the basketball coach.: Bourret, "Digger Phelps and Notre Dame: A Dream Realized."

4   "We were told that . . . thought it was over,": Joe Garner, *et al*, *Echoes of Notre Dame Football* (Naperville, Ill.: Sourcebooks, Inc., 2001), p. 91.

4   After the second half began, . . . temperature rose to normal.: Garner, *et al*, *Echoes of Notre Dame Football*, p. 91.

4   Montana asked Haines if . . . smiled and said, "Let's do it.": Garner, *et al*, *Echoes of Notre Dame Football*, p. 93.

4   When Joe came back . . . was a fairy tale.: Garner, *et al*, *Echoes of Notre Dame Football*, p. 91.

5   Fischer avoided playing for . . . to the Notre Dame campus.: Tim Prister, ed., *What It Means to Be Fighting Irish* (Chicago: Triumph Books, 2004), p. 20.

5   "They were pushing us . . . academy's heavyweight boxing champion.: Prister, *What It Means*, p. 21.

5   I have never regretted it one bit.: Prister, *What It Means*, p. 20.

6   a "one-of-a-kind talent,": Prister, *What It Means*, p. 271.

6   "I don't think I had caught . . . didn't know if I could walk,": Prister, *What It Means*, p. 271.

6   When Ismail entered the game, . . . rookie to try to relax him.: Prister, *What It Means*, p. 272.

6   The ball "hit me in the hands and I dropped it,": Prister, *What It Means*, p. 272.

6   "Son, I told you I didn't . . . exactly what I needed you to do.": Prister, *What It Means*, p. 72.

6   Obviously, things got better from there.: Prister, *What It Means*, p. 272.

7   While making the Dean's List every semester,: "Ruth Riley," *Wikipedia, the free encylopedia*, https://en.wikipedia.org/wiki/Ruth_Riley.

7   "Everybody in the gym knew we . . . throw the ball up,": Dick Patrick, "Riley Ends Notre Dame Career with Title," *USA Today*, April 2, 2001, http://usatoday/30.usatoday.com/sports/basketball/marchmania/2001/womens/stories/2001-04-01-riley-finale.htm#more.

7   "I can't think of a better way to go out,": Patrick, "Riley Ends Notre Dame Career."

7   It's the same play we've . . . 'Get the ball to Ruth.': "Ruth Riley," *Wikipedia, the free encyclopedia*.

8   "the miracle season that saved Notre Dame,": the description is from Jim Dent's book, *Resurrection: The Miracle Season That Saved Notre Dame* (New York City: St. Martin's Press, 2009).

8   Over the summer of 1964, . . . Parseghian caught up with him: Dent, *Resurrection*, p. 170.

8   told him he was his starting . . . and said, "You got it, Coach.": Dent, *Resurrection*, p. 171.

8   There aren't any secrets in coaching.: Jim & Julie S. Bettinger, *The Book of Bowden* (Nashville. TowleHouse Publishing, 2001), p. 31.

9   Florida State showed up at . . . for a history lesson.: Austin Murphy, "Round 1 to the Irish," *SI.com*, Nov. 22, 1993, http://www.si.com/vault/1993/11/22/129948/round-1-to-the-irish.

9   the FSU players talking about . . . they could: a rematch.: Murphy, "Round 1 to the Irish."

9   We're hoping this was just Round 1.: Murphy, "Round 1 to the Irish."

10   In succession, Zaire took three . . . Notre Dame had done all season.: Mary Green, "Split-QB Game Plan Leads to Irish Victory," *The Observer*, Dec. 30, 2014. http://www.ndsmc.observer.com/2014/12/split-qb-game-plan-leads-to-irish-victory/.

10   receiver Chris Brown made his rounds, congratulating both quarterbacks.: Chris Hine, "Cohesive

    Quarterback Tandem Works for Notre Dame in Music City Bowl," *Chicago Tribune*, Dec. 30, 2014, http://www.chicagotribune.com/sports/college/ct-notre-dame-lsu-football-spt-1231-20141230-story.html.

10   This was just utilizing both of their skills to get a win today.: Hine, "Cohesive Quarterback Tandem Works for Notre Dame.

11   Pedro LeLandero grew up in . . . a small fencing club.: "Notre Dame Fencing Springs from Modest Beginnings,"http://publish.netitor.com/photos/schools/nd/sport/c-fenc/auto_pdf/fencing-history.pdf.

11   The program's highlights span . . . and memorable upsets.: "Notre Dame Fencing."

12   Johnson was a quiet, . . . what it was like,": Jerry Barca, *Unbeatable* (New York City: St. Martin's Griffin, 2013), p. 127.

12   "hard-fisted, punch-mouth football.": Joseph Tybor, "Anthony Johnson Quietly Punches Up Irish Offense," *Chicago Tribune*, Sept. 27, 1989, http://www. articles.chicagotribune.com/1989-09-27/sports/8901170654_1_irish-offense-purdue-coach-fred-akers-notre-dame.

12   "If you needed two yards, he'll get it.": Barca, *Unbeatable*, p. 127.

12   I'll tell ya, Anthony Johnson is tough.: Barca, *Unbeatable*, p. 127.

13   The Rev. Michael Shea and . . . and Notre Dame didn't.: Doyle, *Fighting Irish*, p. 49.

13   John brought up the idea . . . go to work on it.": Eric Hansen, *Stadium Stories: Notre Dame Fighting Irish* (Guilford, Conn.: The Globe Pequot Press, 2004), p. 169.

13   Michael Shea later sat . . . of Sacred Heart Church.: Hansen, *Stadium Stories*, p. 170.

13   The "Notre Dame Victory . . . Church in Holyoke.: "Notre Dame Victory March," *UND.com*, http://www.und.com/trads/nd-fightsong.html.

13   John Shea recalled that . . . the administration building.: Hansen, *Stadium Stories*, p. 170.

13   it didn't become a fixture at athletic events until ten years later.: "Notre Dame Victory March.:

13   According to the Notre Dame . . . about 4,000 times a year.: Quoted by Sarah E. Daly, in "For the 16,000 Time . . .," *UND.com*, Oct 8, 2004, http://www.und.com/genrel/100804aaa.html.

13   I wonder if we couldn't work up a pep song [for] Notre Dame.: Hansen, *Stadium Stories*, p. 169.

14   A sophomore at Notre Dame . . . once thought about quitting.": Mike Frank, "Just to Be on the Team," *Scout.com*, July 7, 2005, http://www.scout.com/college/notre-dame/story/393489-just-to-be-on-the-team.

14   In May of 2000, , . . . he never said anything,": Avani Patel, "When Joe Recendez Learned He Needed Surgery," *Chicago Tribune*, Nov. 8, 2000, http://articles.chicagotribune.com/2000=11-08/sports/0011080164_1_testicular-cancer-notre-dame-surgery.

14   he got in for four plays,: Frank, "Just to Be on the Team."

14   108 seconds: Avani Patel, "When Joe Recendez Learned He Needed Surgery.

14   "Absolutely," Recendez said.: Frank, "Just to Be on the Team."

14   For the walk-ons, every single one of us loves Notre Dame.: Frank, "Just to Be on the Team."

15   Before his team's game against . . . They were coaches. They were teachers,": "Brey Coached Despite Mother's Death," *ESPN.go.com*, March 24, 2015, http://espn.go.com/mens-college-basketball/tournament/2015/story/_/id/12548987/notre-dame-coach-mike-brey-never-considered-missing-game.

15   Probably the real driving . . . everything I've done.: "Brey Coached Despite Mother's Death."

16   "played a dang near perfect game for us": Pete Thamel, "Notre Dame's Rout of Texas Confirms Irish Are Better," *SI.com*, Sept. 6, 2015, http://www.si.com/college-football/2015/09/06-notre-dame-fighting-irish-texas-longhorns-malik-zaire.

16   "his first meaningful collegiate playing time.": Eric Hansen, "Backup Quarterback DeShone Kizer Helps Notre Dame," *NDInsider.com*, Sept. 12, 2015, http://www.ndinsider.com/football/backup-quarterback-deshone-kizer-helps-notre-dame-sidestep-upset/article_4d0ad9ca-59be-11e5-8be4-631487bcf9.html.

16   Kizer became a folk hero, . . . forever into Notre Dame lore.: Hansen, "Backup Quarterback."

17   Prior to his senior season, . . . to play both way.: Jon Greenberg, "Touting Trophy's Only All-Chicago Winner," *ESPN.go.com*, Oct. 28, 2011, http://espn.go.com/chicago/ncf/story/_/page/heisman-chicago-week2/john-lattner.

17   He and some other players . . . but we had a ball,": John Heisler, "Then Ara Said to Joe . . . " (Chicago: Triumph Books, 2007), p. 61.

17   She was so delightful. What a gal!: Heisler, "Then Ara Said to Joe . . . ", p. 61.

18   "three of the most . . . in Notre Dame history.": Heisler, "Then Ara Said to Joe . . . ", p. 120

18   Parasegian turned his legendary . . . (such as hair length): Heisler, "Then Ara Said to Joe . . . ", p. 120.

18   In addition to the new . . . Willie Fry, and Al Hunter.: Heisler, "Then Ara Said to Joe . . . ", p. 121.

18   It was unexpected. I thought we were a year away.: Heisler, "Then Ara Said to

Joe . . . ", p. 121.

19   She graduated "as one of the best to ever play under coach Randy Waldrum." Joe Hettler, "Pruzinsky Wins Big East Honor," *The Observer,* Feb. 20, 2004, http://www.ndsmcobserver. com/2004/02/pruzinsky-wins-big-east-honor.

19   she became the first chemical . . . "I'd get distracted.": Chris Ballard, "She's a Kick," *SI.com,* Nov. 17, 2003, http://www.si.com/vault/2013/11/17/354132/she's-a-kick.

19   "For someone so smart, you'd . . . lockers to help her out.: Ballard, "She's a Kick."

19   She can be a little ding-y.: Ballard, "She's a Kick."

20   While the other children . . . offer to lure him.: Todd Burlage, "Overcoming the Odds," *UND.com,* Aug. 29, 2014, http://www.und.com/sports/m-footbl/spec-rel/082914aad.html.

20   It's kind of nice to . . . . prove everyone wrong.: Burlage, "Overcoming the Odds."

21   "an unheard of figure for a pro tackle": David Condon, "Life Is a Party for Czarobski," *Chicago Tribune,* Sept. 15. 1977, http://www.archives.chicagotribune.com/1977/09/15/page/58/article/ life-is-a-party-for-czarobski.

21   on the questionnaire, he . . . his hobbies was "surf-riding": Paul Zimmerman, "The Golden Boys After World War II," *Sports Illustrated,* Nov. 24, 1997, http://www.si.com/vault/1997/11/24/ 235251/the-golden-boys-after-world-war-ii.

21   When he showed up . . . Roosevelt's and Truman's.": Heisler, *"Then Ara Said to Joe . . . ",* p. 39.

21   Everybody has a Ziggy Story.: Zimmerman, "The Golden Boys After World War II."

22   Emotion ran so high for . . . Early. Only 198 Days Left!": Garner, *et al, Echoes of Notre Dame Football,* p. 103.

22   "one of the most hard-fought . . . games in Notre Dame history.": Garner, *et al, Echoes of Notre Dame Football,* p. 105.

22   He was lined up opposite . . . looking to throw the ball his way.": Garner, *et al, Echoes of Notre Dame Football,* p. 107.

22   "With just the very tips of his fingers,": Garner, *et al, Echoes of Notre Dame Football,* p. 107.

22   Irish fans young and . . . beat Miami in 1988.: Garner, *et al, Echoes of Notre Dame Football,* p. 107.

23   Ossello grew up intent on being a college football player: Laura Thomas, "Nick Ossello: Notre Dame Renaissance Man," *UND.com,* Sept. 22, 2015, http://www.und.com/blog/2015/09/nick- ossello-notre-dame-renaissance-man.html.

23   "A fearless midfielder,": Curt Rallo, "Ossello Flips the Switch to Football," *UND.com,* Oct. 28, 2015. http://www.und.com/sports/m-footbl/spec-rel/102815aad.html.

23   "carve[d] out a fierce . . . a relentless force.": Rallo, "Ossello Flips the Switch to Football."

23   in a conversation between Nick . . . the chance to walk on.: Thomas, "Nick Ossello."

23   [Dad and I] thought that was kind of neat.: Thomas, "Nick Ossello."

24   "is considered one of the most . . . the greatest intersectional rivalry": "Notre Dame-USC Football Rivalry," *Wikipedia, The Free Encyclopedia,* https://en.wikipedia.org/wiki/Notre_Dame-USC_ football_rivalry.

24   "the oldest and most . . . rivalry in the country": *Game Day: Notre Dame Football* (Chicago: Triumph Books, 2006), p. 109.

24   the "conversation-between-wives" story.: "Notre Dame-USC Football Rivalry," *Wikpedia.*

24   In 1925, Gwynn Wilson, . . . dead in the water.: *Game Day: Notre Dame Football,* p. 112.

24   Marion Wilson told Bonnie Rockne . . . and the series was on.: *Game Day: Notre Dame Football,* pp. 112-13.

24   If it hadn't been . . . [Notre Dame-Southern Cal] series.: *Game Day: Notre Dame Football,* p. 113.

25   When it ended, Layden . . . "to murmur his apologies.": Doyle, *Fighting Irish,* p. 107.

25   That dang Crimmins!: Doyle, *Fighting Irish,* p. 107.

26   "a breathtaking 6-foot-3 . . . had never wanted to.: Mike Vorel, "Despite Position Change, Carlyle Holiday Still Owns QB Mentality," *South Bend Tribune,* Aug. 3, 2015, http://www.ndinsider. com/football/despite-position-change-and-career-move-carlyle-holiday-still-owns/article_ 6929ea26-3a27-11e5-8455-bbe89df3291e.html.

26   "I had been playing . . . he would have left,: Vorel, "Despite Position Change."

27   "the best player I had over my Notre Dame career.": Phelps with Bourret, p. 146.

27   The award stemmed from an . . . by the broken glass.: Phelps with Bourret, pp. 122-23.

27   Despite a severe injury . . . he had saved Rivers' life.: Phelps with Bourret, p. 123.

27   Rivers underwent several hours . . . the debris out of his stomach.: Phelps with Bourret, p. 147.

27   he was back in class by . . . were twisting his bowels.: Phelps with Bourret, p. 147.

27   Fittingly, David Rivers accepted . . . room over the phone.: Phelps with Bourret, p. 147.

28   Leahy believed that games were . . . until their hands bled.: "Frank Leahy," *Wikipedia, the free encyclopedia,* http://en.wikipedia.org/wiki/Frank_Leahy.

28   Leahy astounded everyone by . . . in the fourth quarter": Gildea and Jennison, p. 64.

28   We looked across the field . . . we would have been.: Gildea and Jennison, p. 64.
29   Minutes before the team . . . monumental significance for them.: John Heisler, "Sunday Brunch:
          Nobody Better at Home," *UND.com*, Nov. 15, 2015, http://www.und.com/sports/m-footbl/
          spec-rel/111515aaa.html.
29   "The final numbers were . . . all-time winningest class": Heisler, "Sunday Brunch: Nobody Better."
29   After the post-game . . . a victory lap.: Heisler, "Sunday Brunch: Nobody Better."
29   You've left a legacy.: Heisler, "Sunday Brunch: Nobody Better."
30   "the most important two weeks in the pre-Rockne era,": Gildea and Jennison, p. 22.
30   "a revelation to the Pittsburgh . . . adept at the modern game.": Gildea and Jennison, p. 24.
30   the Pitt fans politely . . . that officials didn't count.": Doyle, *Fighting Irish*, p. 48.
30   The Michigan head coach tried . . . school officials praising the team.: Gildea and Jennison, p. 24.
30   Notre Dame, by defeating . . . for the title in this section.; Gildea and Jennison, p. 24.
31   Haley Scott DeMaria knows that hope can be sorely tested.": "Bus Crash Survivors [*sic*] Offers
          Hope to Others," *ESPN.go.com*, June 5, 2008, http://sports.espn.go.com/espn/wire?id=3428054.
31   Most of the other survivors . . . a broken back,: Dennis Brown, "Alumna Haley Scott DeMaria,"
          Notre Dame News, March 28, 2012, http://news.nd.edu/news/29908-alumna-haley-scott-
          demaria-to-deliver-2012-notre-dame-commencement-address.
31   "All I knew was that I was cold and my back hurt,": Janelle Goodwin, "Defying Diagnosis, Notre
          Dame Alum Walks," *CatholicPhilly.com*, Oct. 30, 2015. http://catholicphilly.com/2015/10/news/
          local-news/defying-diagnosis-swimmer-walks-and-swims-again-after-horrific-crash/
31   After two operations, : Brown, "Alumna Haley Scott DeMaria."
31   Five days after the accident, . . . cane and walked on her own.: "Bus Crash Survivors."
31   She returned to classes at Notre Dame that fall: Brown, "Alumna Haley Scott DeMaria."
31   and graduated only one semester behind her classmates.: Goodwin, "Defying Diagnosis."
31   In the summer of 1992, . . . 50-yard freestyle race.: Brown, "Alumna Haley Scott DeMaria."
31   her faith and her desire to honor her fallen teammates.: Goodwin, "Defying Diagnosis."
31   Keep praying. God listens.: Goodwin, "Defying Diagnosis."
32   a preposterous 56-yard field goal.: Garner, *et al, Echoes of Notre Dame Football*, p. 53.
32   Syracuse fans rushed the field to celebrate their victory.: "Notre Dame vs. Syracuse, 11/18/1961,"
          University of Notre Dame Archives, www.archives.nd.edu/about/news/index.php/2011/nd-vs-
          syracuse-11181961/#.VEAfVPnF-So.
32   Syracuse's athletic director . . . gave up the fight.: Garner, *et al, Echoes of Notre Dame Football*, p. 53.
32   There's the kick. And . . . is through? It's good!: Garner, *et al, Echoes of Notre Dame Football*, p. 53
33   After a 33-0 steamrolling of Pittsburgh . . . one third-string guard: Bob McBride.: Michael Rodio,
          "More Than a Game," *Notre Dame Magazine*, Summer 2012, http://magazine.nd.edu/news/
          31345-more-than-a-game/.
33   [Bob] McBride was an . . . unyielding determination to succeed.: Rodio, "More Than a Game."
34   In the spring of 1913, . . . fourteen sets of cleat: Hansen, *Stadium Stories*, p. 23.
34   Army had scouted Notre . . . any of his linemen.: Hansen, *Stadium Stories*, p. 16.
34   Quarterback Gus Dorais and . . . practiced throwing the football.: Hansen, *Stadium Stories*, p. 17.
34   Games of the day were . . . brute strength and line plunges.": Hansen, *Stadium Stories*, p. 16.
34   Notre Dame "threw it . . . totally confounded" Army's defense.: Hansen, *Stadium Stories*, p. 16.
34   The win "spread the school's name across the country.": Hansen, *Stadium Stories*, p. 24.
34   It also changed the . . . as a viable offensive option.: Hansen, *Stadium Stories*,, p. 17.
34   On the way home, . . . big breakfast -- on Syracuse.: Hansen, *Stadium Stories*, p. 23.
34   I was just happy we . . . ahead on the deal.: Hansen, *Stadium Stories*, p. 16.
35   "like a fullback in football,": Bruce Newman, "The Master of Disaster," *Sports Illustrated*, Jan. 19,
          1981, http://www.si.com/vault/1981/01/19/825294/the-master-of-disaster.
35   once score 56 points . . . trying to kill each other.: Newman, "The Master of Disaster."
35   We weren't the Waltons and it wasn't all lovey-dovey.: Newman, "The Master of Disaster."
36   "I guess I just like . . . to return to California.: Marty Burns, "Lyron Cobbins," *SI.com*, Aug. 1, 1966,
          http://www.si.com/vault/1996/08/01/216918/lyron-cobbins.
36   I don't get off campus much.: Burns, "Lyron Cobbins."
37   "We knew we were lacking . . . just too much to replace.": Prister, *What It Means*, p. 161.
37   "There was a lot of sentiment . . . between the coaches and players.": Prister, *What It Means*, p. 161.
37   The coaches' wives and their . . . "It was kind of strange,": Prister, *What It Means*, pp. 161-62.
37   It was free will and we exercised the right to choose.: Prister, *What It Means*, p. 161.
38   The Lord works in mysterious ways.": Tim Layden, "Modern Irish," *SI.com*, Nov. 26, 2012,
          http://www.si.com/vault/2012/11/26/106258863/modern-irish.
38   the day "had turned black . . . unbeaten season seemingly finished.: Layden,
          "Modern Irish."
38   "Our team kept fighting, kept playing,": "Notre Dame Rallies to Outlast Upset-

Minded Pitt," *ESPN.go.com*, Nov. 4, 2012, http://scores.espn.go.com/ncf/recap?gameId= 323080087.

39   "Her passion [for the game] makes her . . . are [still] the most exciting," Curt Rallo, "Jewell's Drive," *UND.com*, March 17, 2015, http://www.und.com/sports/w-baskbl/spec-rel/031715aaa.html.

39   She always wanted to be around basketball.: Rallo, "Jewell's Drive."

40   Terry Brennan had spotted . . . were running five plays.": Garner, *et al*, *Echoes of Notre Dame Football*, pp. 41-42

40   Knowing his defense . . . into the backfield.: Garner, *et al*, *Echoes of Notre Dame Football*, p. 42.

40   80 yards away "from football destiny.": Doyle, *Fighting Irish*, p. 145.

40   Irish cocaptain Ed Sullivan . . . the game ended.: Garner, *et al*, *Echoes of Notre Dame Football*, p. 43.

40   A three-touchdown underdog . . . much from Notre Dame.: Garner, *et al*, *Echoes of Notre Dame Football*, p. 41.

41   Irish athletic director Moose . . . wasn't too far away.: Hansen, *Stadium Stories*, p. 88.

41   thousands of fans without . . . to South Bend police.: Hansen, *Stadium Stories*, p. 93.

41   "the recent death of . . . Diana, Princess of Wales.: Hansen, *Stadium Stories* , p. 90.

41   a combination of design . . . and outdated commodes": Hansen, *Stadium Stories*, p. 74.

41   Water from dozens of . . . close down fifteen concession stands.: Hansen, *Stadium Stories*, p. 73.

41   It also led to $4 million . . . that took four years to clear up.: Hansen, *Stadium Stories*, p. 74.

41   The day turned so muggy . . . treated for heat exhaustion.: Hansen, *Stadium Stories*, p. 73.

41   There's a certain amount . . . project of that magnitude.: Hansen, *Stadium Stories*, p. 74.

42   He decided it was time . . . and find his own way.": Todd Burlage, "A Twist of Fate Leads Sanford Through Coaching Ranks," *UND.com*, Oct. 19, 2015. http://www.und.com/sports/m-footbl/ spec-rel/101915aae.html.

42   In December, the news broke . . . flight selling himself.: Burlage, "A Twist of Fate."

42   Every job [I've] had a chance to get came out of that meeting.: Burlage, "A Twist of Fate."

43   Irish head coach Digger Phelps . . . "one of my best walk-ons.": Phelps with Bourret, p. 133.

43   Kelly was from Los Angeles, . . . roles of the opposing team.: Phelps with Bourret, pp. 132-33.

43   Kelly agreed to do it . . . theater in rambunctious celebration.: Phelps with Bourret, p. 133.

44   The Irish equipment manager . . . "So thirteens it was.": Hansen, *Stadium Stories*, p. 42.

44   On Hart's recruiting visit . . . over any ill feelings: Hansen, *Stadium Stories*, pp. 42-43.

44   "His arrest was a betrayal . . . a travesty of justice.": Charles Swindoll, "Analysis of a Courtroom Fiasco," *Sermon Series: Jesus: The Greatest Life of All*, http://daily. insight.org/site/News2?page= NewsArticle&id=9653.

44   [Coaches] 'Moose' Krause and . . . take good care of him.: Hansen, *Stadium Stories*, p. 43.

45   one of "the iconic memories of modern Irish lore.": Keith Arnold, " Irish Memories: Reggie Brooks and the Snow Bowl," *NBC Sports*, March 17, 2011, http://irish.nbcsports.com/2011/03/17/irish-memories-reggie-brooks-and-the-snow-bowl/.

45   from a formation Notre Dame had never run.: John Heisler, *Greatest Moments in Notre Dame Football History* (Chicago: Triumph Books, 2008), p. 104.

45   Having already been booed . . . going for the tie.: "November 14, 1992 — The Snow Bowl," *TodayinNDHistory.com*, http://www.todayinndhistory.com/pages/events/?id=391.

45   Holtz went for two and ad-libbed a play on the sideline.: Arnold, "Irish Memories."

45   A winter squall had descended . . . stadium, blanketing the field white.: "November 14, 1992."

46   "has emerged as one of [the school's] most visible and consistently elite programs.": Pete LaFleur, "Celebrating 25 Years of Excellence," *UND.com*, Oct. 18, 2012, http://www.und.com/sports/ w-soccer/spec-rel/101812aaa.html.

46   The first varsity squad featured . . . it was not great soccer,": LaFleur, "Celebrating 25 Years."

46   Before the game, the head . . . score the winning goal.: "Leon Lifts #7/10 Notre Dame to NCAA Title," *UND.com*, Dec. 5, 2010, http://www.und.com/sports/w-soccer/recaps/120510aaa.html.

46   I teased Adriana [Leon] before . . . the game winner today.': "NCAA Championship Game Postgame Quotes," *UND.com*, Dec. 5, 2010, http://www.und.com/sports/w-soccer-recaps/120510 aaf.html.

47   The team interrupted its train ride . . . predicted an easy USC win.: Gildea and Jennison, p. 42.

47   With everyone looking on, . . . "Rock, you can't leave us now.": Gildea and Jennison, p. 42.

47   I'm finished with you. I'm . . . the stands for the second half. Gildea and Jennison, p. 40.

48   Just days before the 1978 . . . it won't be a squeaker.": Joe Garner, *et al*, *Echoes of Notre Dame Football*, p. 87.

48   Devine quickly made it . . . else out of him.: Garner, *et al*, *Echoes of Notre Dame Football*, p. 87.

48   "The game was over right there.": quoted by Heisler, *Greatest Moments in Notre Dame Football History*, p. 50.

48   I just had to . . . I was right all along.: Garner, *et al*, *Echoes of Notre Dame Football*, p. 89.

49   Walton's only football offer . . . could give football a try.: Keith Arnold, "Catching Up with . . . Shane Walton," *Inside the Irish*, Sept. 24, 2009, http://irish.nbcsports.com/2009/09/24/catching-up-with-shane-walton/.

49   He discovered that playing . . . club experience had been.: Matthew DeFranks, "Shane Walton Moves from Soccer to Coaching," *The Observer*, Sept. 26, 2013, http://www.ndsmcobserver.com/2013/09/shane-walton-moves-from-soccer-to-coaching/.

49   "I don't know if he . . . was the toughest challenge.: Arnold, "Catching Up With . . . Shane Walton."

49   That process took about a year to really transform.: Arnold, "Catching Up With . . . Shane Walton."

50   there can be only one . . . Austin Carr, Class of 1971.": Lou Somogyi, "Austin Carr Enters The Ring," *notredame247sports.com*, Feb. 26, 2011, http://notredame.247sports.com/Article/Austin-Carr-Notre-Dames-Greatest-Ever-In-Basketball-16497.

50   what has been called "the golden age of scorers.": Somogyi, "Austin Carr."

50   One researcher reviewed the . . . would have scored 73 points.: "Sweet 61: Carr's Tourney Scoring Record Stands Test of Time," *UND.com*, March 26, 2015, http://www.und.com/sports/m-baskbl/spec-real/032615aaf.html.

50   With the way the game is . . . Called "the unguardable guard,".: "Sweet 61."

50   It's a good feeling to have the record. I'm amazed it has lasted [this] long.: "Sweet 61."

51   Rassas turned down thirteen . . . and rebounder, fouled out.: Dent, *Resurrection*, p. 32.

51   For two seasons, he was never promoted past the fifth string.: Dent, *Resurrection*, p. 33.

51   He was considered so . . . report to preseason camp.: Dent, *Resurrection*, p. 34.

51   Only an angry letter from . . . him to the team.: Dent, *Resurrection*, p. 35.

51   Rassas was buried on what . . . the Grotto and say a prayer.: Dent, *Resurrection*, pp. 36-37.

51   The next day, Rassas walked . . . and forgot about it.: Dent, *Resurrection*, p. 38.

51   Several weeks later, Devore sat . . . to first string on the spot.: Dent, *Resurrection*, pp. 40-41.

51   I need some help here. . . . you can make it fast.: Dent, *Resurrection*, p. 38.

52   Leahy was either a defector . . . whenever you want. Good-bye.": Todd Burlage, "Frank Leahy: A Coach for Two Schools," *UND.com*, Nov. 17, 2015, http://www.und.com/sports/m-footbl/spec-rel/111715aaa.html.

52   People were riled when Leahy left.: Burlage, "Frank Leahy."

53   they went 7:35 without . . . and rebounder, fouled out.: John Fineran, "Notre Dame Squeaks by South Carolina," *South Bend Tribune*, April 6, 2015, http://www.ndinsider.com/basketball/womens/notre-dame-squeaks-by-south-carolina.

53   with 1:12 left, South Carolina completed . . . first of the game.: Al Lesar, "Notre Dame's Unlikely Heroes Embrace Moment," *South Bend Tribune*, April 5, 2015, http://www.ndinsider.com/basketball/womens/notre-dame-s-unlikely-heroes.

53   She "slashed in from nowhere," . . . knew it [would be] short.": Lesar, "Notre Dame's Unlikely Heroes Embrace Moment."

53   Hannah Huffman, who played . . . top of the backboard.: Lesar, "Notre Dame's Unlikely Heroes Embrace Moment."

53   Things couldn't have looked bleaker for No. 2 Notre Dame.: Fineran, ""Notre Dame Squeaks by South Carolina."

54   McKenna had been injured . . . to the travel squad.: Garner, *et al*, *Echoes of Notre Dame Football*, p. 27.

54   Carrying his uniform,: Doyle, *Fighting Irish*, p. 104.

54   he sneaked onto the . . . in a teammate's berth: Garner, *et al*, *Echoes of Notre Dame Football*, p. 27.

54   He called the signals, . . . a heavier Buckeye defender.: Garner, *et al*, *Echoes of Notre Dame Football*, p. 27.

54   Up came backfield coach [Chet] Grant, tugging along [Jim] McKenna.: Doyle, *Fighting Irish*, p. 104.

55   "Theismann's skill and confidence . . . was drafted either.: Prister, *What It Means*, p. 152.

55   Theismann weighed 152 pounds. . . really wanted to play ball.": Prister, *What It Means*, p. 148.

55   One visit to North . . . with beautiful women around,": Prister, *What It Means*, p. 149.

55   I went out on two dates my first two years at Notre Dame.: Prister, *What It Means*, p. 149.

56   Male "could have been Rudy.": Heisler, "*Then Ara Said to Joe . . .*", p. 146.

56   Male was kicking by . . . and you need equipment.: Heisler, "*Then Ara Said to Joe . . .*", p. 146.

56   Coach Devine would tell . . . a continent or something.: Heisler, "*Then Ara Said to Joe . . .*", p. 146.

57   As the youngest of the . . . older brothers' wrestling moves.: Devon Heinen, "Saving Best for Last at Notre Dame," *ESPN.go.com*, April 23, 2013, http://espn.go.com/lacrosse/story/_id/9185534/lacrosse-notre-dame-goalie-john-kemp-carries-family-tradition.

57   An older brother gave up . . . target practice for Joey.: Heinen, "Saving Best for Last."

57   John kinda had no choice.: Heinen, "Saving Best for Last."

58   The team acquired its . . . Kill those Fighting Irish!": Doyle, *Fighting Irish*, p. 35.

58   interest in the sport had . . . team captain filled the post.: Doyle, *Fighting Irish*, pp. 36-37.

58   Irish football took off after . . . at Michigan the previous year.: Doyle, *Fighting Irish*, p. 37.
58   He was paid $40,.: Chantel Jennings, "Linked History Preserves a Rivalry," *ESPN.go.com*, Sept. 6,
      2013, http://www.espn.go.com/college-football/story/_/id/9640386/the-historic-notre-dame-
      michigan-rivalry-never-really-gone.
58   Frank E. Hering, the man . . . "from the school's farm.: Doyle, *Fighting Irish*, p. 37.
59   It took Jarrett Grace 22 months to finally play football pain free.": J.J. Stankevitz, "Finally Pain Free,
      Jarrett Grace Ready to Return," *CSNCHICAGO.com*, Aug. 16, 2015, http://www.csnchicago.
      com/notre-dame-finally-ready-return-notre-dame.
59   "a devastating injury." . . . that's a driving factor.": Curt Rallo, "Jarrett Grace's Long Road to
      Recovery," *UND.com*, April 15, 2015, http://www.und.com/sports/m-football/spec-rel/
      041515aaa.html.
59   I like having bruises . . . from football anytime.: Rallo, "Jarrett Grace's Long Road."
60   Greatest collection of college football talent in history.": Zimmerman, "The Golden Boys After
      World War II."
60   Phil Colella, the second-leading . . . making the coaches' decisions easier.: Zimmerman, "The
      Golden Boys After World War II."
60   "The best games [of the season] will be the intrasquad scrimmages at South Bend.": Tom Siler in *Pic
      Magazine* and quoted by Paul Zimmerman, "The Golden Boys After World War II."
60   For sheer talent, nothing could match our teams of '46 and '47.: Zimmerman, "The Golden Boys
      After World War II."
61   The first thing he noticed . . . didn't have a prayer.": Garner, *et al*, *Echoes of Notre Dame Football*, p. 96.
61   "It was as if Mother . . . Jesus just in time,": Garner, *et al*, *Echoes of Notre Dame Football*, p. 96.
61   Bill Siewe made the . . . like a good golf swing.: Garner, *et al*, *Echoes of Notre Dame Football*, p. 97.
61   Well, it's miracle time for Notre Dame.: Garner, *et al*, *Echoes of Notre Dame Football*, p. 95.
62   Notre Dame assistant coach Frank . . . you scouted teams in person," Phelps with Bourret, p. 74.
62   Before the game, Phelps walked . . . what was going on.: Phelps with Bourret, p. 75.
62   Before he left LA, . . . send in tapes of opponents.: Phelps with Bourret, p. 75.
62   I was sold on its value. We would have paid $5,000 for it.: Phelps with Bourret, p. 75.
63   his dad was a fan . . . Academy, Arizona, and Cincinnati.: Samantha Zuba, "Unfinished Business:
      Joe Schmidt," *The Observer*, Nov. 20, 2014, http://ndsmc.observer.com/2014/11/unfinished-
      business-joe-schmidt.
63   Notre Dame's coaches had no . . . guy off that we want.": Tom Coyne, "Notre Dame Linebacker
      Schmidt Goes from Walk-On to Captain," *MSN.com*, Oct. 8, 2015, http://www.msn.com/en-
      us-sports-ncaafb-notre-dame-linebacker-schmidt-goes-from-walk-on-to-captain/ar-
      AAffRdg?ocid=U221DHP.
63   On Twitter, Schmidt let . . . thank you God.": Bob Kollars, "Joe Schmidt and the Spirit of Notre
      Dame," *UHND.com*, June 16, 2013, http://www.uhnd.com/articles/football/spirit-notre-dame/.
63   if Rudy Ruettiger got a . . . a pretty cool story.": Coyne, "Notre Dame Linebacker."
63   As a kid, my dream was always to play at Notre Dame.: Zuba, "Unfinished Business."
64   As a child, Becton had . . . practice player for the Irish.": William F. Reed, "Lee Becton: Cotton,"
      Sports Illustrated, Jan. 10, 1994, http://www.si.com/vault/1994/01/10/130229/lee-becton-cotton.
64   "I didn't think he could . . . got ready to take over.: Reed, "Lee Becton: Cotton."
64   I never dreamed about getting 100 yards.: Reed, "Lee Becton: Cotton."
65   "We were out of business during World War II,": Lou Somogyi, "The Ties That Bind," *UND.com*,
      Oct. 27, 2011, http://www.UND.com/sports/m-footbl/spec-rel/102711aah.html?wappref=std.
65   To alleviate the desperate . . . as Navy wanted it.: Somogyi, "The Ties That Bind."
65   Despite the one-sided result . . . for historical reasons.: "Navy-Notre Dame Football Rivalry,"
      Wikipedia, the free encyclopedia, http://en.wikipedia.org/wiki/Navy-Notre_Dame_football_
      rivalry.
66   The foundation for Bertelli's win . . . from sea to shining sea.: "Angelo Bertelli," *UHND.com*, http://
      www.uhnd.com/history/heismans/angelo-bertelli/.
66   "In the biggest arena . . . Bertelli was the clear star.: "Angelo Bertelli," *UHND.com*.
66   Aware of the scourge of . . . wear a football uniform.: "Angelo Bertelli, *UHND.com*.
67   In the late 1980s, the . . . the college football landscape.: Jerry Barca, "Notre Dame-Miami Rivalry
      Dominated College Football Landscape," *UND.com*, Oct. 5, 2012, http://www.und.com/
      genrel/100512aae.html.
67   Irish quarterback Rick Mirer, who at the time accounted for more points running and throwing
      (350) than other player in Notre Dame history,: "Rick Mirer," *Wikipedia, the free encyclopedia*,
      https://en.wikipedia.org/wiki/Rick_Mirer.
67   "The Miami rivalry brought out the best in us.": Barca, "Notre Dame-Miami Rivalry Dominated
      College Football Landscape."

67 Over the morning meal . . . their helmets in acknowledgement.: Barca, "Notre Dame-Miami Rivalry Dominated College Football Landscape."

67 Rick Mirer helped seal Miami's fate over a plate of breakfast.: Barca, "Notre Dame-Miami Rivalry Dominated College Football Landscape."

68 Notre Dame quarterback Tom Clements was so surprised by the call that he actually flinched.: Garner, *et al, Echoes of Notre Dame Football*, p. 75.

68 "I think it was the . . . call didn't surprise me.": Garner, *et al, Echoes of Notre Dame Football*, p. 75.

68 his second reception of the season.: Heisler, *Greatest Moments in Notre Dame Football History* , p. 42.

68 That pass really caught us by surprise.: Garner, *et al, Echoes of Notre Dame Football*, p. 77.

69 From 1918-30, Knute Rockne was . . . various points in between.": Hansen, *Stadium Stories*, p. 74.

69 The powers that be were . . . size that Rockne envisioned.: Hansen, *Stadium Stories*, p. 79.

69 Threatening to go coach at other schools,: Hansen, *Stadium Stories*, p. 80.

69 It came complete with the . . . insisted be transplanted.: Hansen, *Stadium Stories*, p. 82.

69 Almost everyone was sober.: Hansen, *Stadium Stories*, p. 84.

70 She was such a devastating . . . their block against her.: Pete LaFleur, "Andrea McHugh: Freedom Through Faith," *UND.com*, Nov. 5, 2013, http://www.und.com/sports/w-volley/spec-rel/110513aae.html.

70 McHugh grew up in a . . . found a sport she loved,": LaFleur, "Andrea McHugh."

70 Jeff McHugh's head had been . . . in his own backyard.: LaFleur, "Andrea McHugh."

71 "one of the most productive running backs in Notre Dame history.": Todd Burlage, "Prosise's Journey from Good to Great," *UND.com*, Dec. 10, 2015, http://www.und.com/sports/m-footbl/spec-rel/121015aac.html.

71 He was just fooling around . . . but we've got to take him.'": Burlage, "Prosise's Journey."

71 the coaches decided that he didn't backpedal very well,: Alex Carson, "Prosise Runs His Way into Notre Dame Record Books," *The Observer*, Sept. 22, 2015, http://ndsmcobserver.com/2015/09/football-teleconference-wrap/.

71 We've just got to find a place for [C.J. Prosise] to play.: Burlage, "Prosise's Journey."

72 the biggest Heisman-Trophy winner of all time.: "Leon Hart, *UHND.com*, http://unhd.com/history/heismans/leon-hart/.

72 Twenty years after Hart's . . . and weighed 210 pounds.: "Leon Hart," *UHND.com*.

72 eight Southern Cal lads had . . . and left them for dead.: "Leon Hart," *UHND.com*.

73 The single game [of the Dan . . . people's minds is the victory": Doyle, *Fighting Irish*, p. 193.

73 The Irish wore their traditional . . . the pre-game warmups: Doyle, *Fighting Irish*, p. 193.

73 Back in the locker room, . . . "steamed onto the field": Doyle, *Fighting Irish*, p. 195.

73 On Oct. 8, 1921, Knute Rockne . . . into the green uniforms.: Ismail, "The Green Machine: A History of Notre Dame's Green Jerseys," *BleacherReport.com*, March 9, 2010, http://www.bleacherreport.com/articles/359516-the-green-machine-a-history-of-notre-dames-green-jerseys.

73 The traditional blue jerseys took . . . his team up in exclusively green.": Ismail.

73 It will be remembered forever as 'the Green Jersey Game.': Doyle, *Fighting Irish*, p. 195.

74 some pickup games the summer . . . finesse to his game.: Luke Winn, "Going Gaga for 'Gody," *SI.com*, March 17, 2008, http://www.si.com/vault/2008,03/17/104581281/going-gaga-for-gody.

74 With a month, Brey . . . "It's about time.": Winn, "Going Gaga for 'Gody."

74 At least I'm going to get a degree from a great university.: Winn, "Going Gaga for 'Gody."

75 His mom once observed of her son, "He loves the stage.": Stewart Mandel, "Show Stopper," *Sports Illustrated*, Sept. 20, 2004, http://www.si.com/vault/2004/09/20/8185824/show-stopper.

75 When he returned to . . . humbling thing I had ever seen.": Mike Monaco, "Waking the Echoes: Darius Walker," *The Observer*, Sept. 25, 2014, http://ndsmcobserver.com/2014/09/waking-echoes-darius-walker/.

75 It was my induction into . . . that is Notre Dame football.: Monaco, "Waking the Echoes."

76 Math professor and baseball . . . to help coach the team.: Doyle, *Fighting Irish*, p. 116.

76 The only starter left from the 1943 team was guard Pat Filley.: Doyle, *Fighting Irish*, p. 118.

76 Few freshmen in 1946 would . . . have lost a single game.: Doyle, *Fighting Irish*, p. 121.

77 Paul Hornung's path to the . . . intrigue, surprise, and adventure.": "Paul Hornung," *UHND.com*, http://www.unhd.com/history/heismans/paul-hornung.

77 He was "personable, dashing, . . . midst of gridiron battle.": "Paul Hornung," *UHND.com*.

77 the week after Michigan . . . won the Heisman Trophy.: "Paul Hornung," *UHND.com*.

77 For decades, wags [said] . . . Paul Hornung's name on it.: "Paul Hornung," *UHND.com*.

78 Before football, students competed . . . of all things — marbles!: Doyle, *Fighting Irish*, p. 33.

78 Notre Dame's first football All- . . . moved right into the lineup.: Doyle, *Fighting Irish*, p. 42.

78 each of the eleven . . . was from a different state.: Doyle, *Fighting Irish*, p. 34.

78 The first Indiana player, . . . a touchdown should be allowed.: Doyle, *Fighting Irish*, p. 35.

78   In 1889, upset by the injuries . . . talked him out of it.: Doyle, *Fighting Irish*, p. 36.
79   Growing up in Pennsylvania, . . . legendary high school coach.: Prister, *What It Means*, p. 70.
79   He weighed all of 155 pounds when he graduated from high school: Prister, *What It Means*, p. 75.
79   a local guy was one of . . . the dorms, met the coaches,: Prister, *What It Means*, p. 70.
79   played some basketball while . . . though, McBride was there.: Prister, *What It Means*, p. 71
79   "I knew I could work harder than anybody else.": Prister, *What It Means*, p. 74.
79   They were kind of backing away from me because of my size.: Prister, *What It Means*, p. 71.
80   Beuerlein figured his college . . . coach after the 1985 season.: Jerry Barca, *Unbeatable*, p. 59.
80   He also knew Holtz preferred . . . Then he would be benched.: Barca, *Unbeatable*, pp. 59-60.
80   "I've already given you the . . . You will not regret it,": Barca, *Unbeatable*, p. 60.
80   Get your butt back out there and go win us the football game.: Barca, *Unbeatable*, p. 60.
81   They declared themselves insulted . . . after the Wolverines' win.: Matt Fortuna, "Irish Deliver
        Final Blow in Michigan Rivalry," *ESPN.go com*, Sept. 7, 2014, http://www.espn.go.com/blog/
        ncfnation/post/_/id/98314-irish-deliver-final-blow-in-michigan-rivalry.
81   Normally quite level-headed, starting . . . Hey Hey Kiss Him Goodbye.": Fortuna, "Irish Deliver
        Final Blow in Michigan Rivalry."
81   Notre Dame flat-out demoralized . . . the programs' last meeting.: Fortuna, "Irish Deliver Final
        Blow in Michigan Rivalry."
82   She spent much of her freshman . . . the way Seidel trained.: John A. Kissane, "Molly Seidel: 'I've
        Been Hearing about That Stupid Curse for Years,'" *RunnersWorld.com*, Nov. 24, 2015. http://
        www.runnersworld.com/college/molly-seidel-ive-been-hearing-about-that-stupid-curse-
        for-years."
82   Seidel had an accident on her bike and "busted up" her knee.: Kissane, "Molly Seidel."
82`   I've been hearing about that stupid curse for years.: Kissane, "Molly Seidel."
83   When Hanratty called her after . . . should try to be like him.: Prister, *What It Means*, p. 140.
83   Hanratty and Seymour often . . . could catch it anywhere,": Prister, *What It Means*, p. 138.
83   It was during the third offensive . . . to be a halfback draw!": Prister, *What It Means*, pp. 140-41.
83   I couldn't figure out why Ara would call for [a quarterback draw].: Prister, *What It Means*, p. 140.
84   In 1992, Chryplewicz was a struggling, . . . huddle the next play,": Prister, *What It Means*, p. 299.
84   "It was a long, hard . . . wanted to play for.: Prister, *What It Means*, p. 299.
84   Then the coach went to . . . for you this Saturday.": Prister, *What It Means*, p. 300.
84   I was just floored! My heart dropped, my stomach ached.: Prister, *What It Means*, p. 300.
85   The Old Fieldhouse was built . . . to render it fireproof.: Dent, *Resurrection*, p. 13.
85   The building had a clay . . . were also held there.: "Postcard Views of Notre Dame," *IrishLegends.
        com*, http://www.irishlegends.com/Pages/postcard/postcard_nov01.htm. The material on
        the website is lifted from *The University of Notre Dame: A Portrait of Its History and Campus* by
        Thomas Schlereth.
85   Beginning on Friday evenings in the 1920s,: Dent, *Resurrection*, p. 13.
85   "a pressurized capsule of cacophony.": "Postcard Views of Notre Dame."
85   The gatherings were "so . . . farms that ringed campus.": Dent, *Resurrection*, p. 13.
85   The students jammed the . . . circus without the elephants.": Dent, *Resurrection*, p. 14.
85   The Irish had been tied . . . "I know. I timed it,": Dent, *Resurrection*, p. 14.
85   [Father Morrissey] had no way of . . . center of Notre Dame athletics.: Dent, *Resurrection*, p. 13.
86   I don't know that we'll ever have another player like her.": Ann Hardie, "Being Skylar Diggins,"
        Notre Dame Magazine, Winter 2012-13, http://magazine.nd.edu/news/36628-being-skylar-
        diggins/.
86   McGraw offered Diggins . . . done anything like that.: Richard Deitsch, "Win One for the Home
        Team," *Sports Illustrated*, Nov. 14, 2011, http://www.si.com/vault/2011/11/14/106130688/
        win-one-for-the-home-team.
86   Diggins didn't arrive at . . . gibe it up.": Graham Hays, "Diggins 'Owns the Day' in Record Win,"
        espnW.com, March 31, 2013, http://espn.go.com/womens-college-basketball/tournament/
        2013/story/_-id/9117457/womens-ncaa-tournament-2013-skylar-diggins-hoops-mastery-
        record-setting-game.
86   Diggins is a self- . . . an 11 p.m. curfew.: Deitsch, "Win One for the Home Team."
86   her Twitter account had . . . male or female.: Scoop Jackson, "The Skylar Diggins Balancing Act,"
        ESPN.go.com, Dec. 23, 2011, http://espn.go.com/espn/commentary/story/_/page/jackson-
        111223/skylar-diggins-notre-dame-balances-beauty-athleticism.
86   In high school, when . . . the time she was nine: Deitsch, "Win One for the Home Team."
86   she started all but . . . to start on Senior Day.: Mackenzie Kruvant, "18 Things You Should Actually
        Know about Skylar Diggins," *BuzzFeed*, July 17, 2014, http://www.buzzfeed.com/mackenzie
        kruvant/things-you-should-actually-know-about-skylar-diggins#.xfgAYPdZKA.

87   All week long before the . . . "Notre Dame: They're fat slobs.": Skip Myslenski, "Notre Dame Goes
      Kicking into the Cotton," *SI.com*, Nov. 30, 1970, http://www.si.com/vault/1970/11/30/611874/
      notre-dame-goes-kicking-into-the-cotton.
87   "humiliating. I've never been . . . this week I am.": Myslenski, "Notre Dame Goes Kicking."
87   "If they want to make it . . . one could hope to see.": Myslenski, "Notre Dame Goes Kicking."
87   When Jim Yoder punted . . . you believe 2-nothin'?": Myslenski, "Notre Dame Goes Kicking."
87   I've never been called a slob in my life.: Myslenski, "Notre Dame Goes Kicking."
88   On May 22, 2013, Ohio State and . . . through a half-hour throwing session.": David Briggs, "Golden
      Opportunity," *The Blade*, Dec. 20, 2015, http://www.bcsn.tv/news_article/show/591298.
88   "It looked like the Wild . . . going to offer Kizer a scholarship.: Briggs, "Golden Opportunity."
88   You could tell he was really pressing, and we've all seen that.: Briggs, "Golden Opportunity."
89   Wednesday before the game, . . . but they did it.: Phelps with Bourret, p. 24.
89   Notre Dame forced UCLA into . . . elegant play turned crude.": Barry McDermott, "After 88 Comes
      Zero," *SI.com*, Jan. 28, 1974, http://www.si.com/vault/1974/01/28/617039/after-88-comes-zero.
89   the students rushed the . . . messed up the whole day,": Phelps with Bourret, p. 34.
89   You couldn't underestimate the importance of confidence when you were playing UCLA.: Phelps
      with Bourret, p. 25.
90   His offense was missing ten . . . Frank Allocco separated his shoulder.: John Underwood, "The
      Echoes Are Wide Awake," *Sports Illustrated*, Sept. 29, 1975, http://www.si.com/vault/1975/
      09/29/606782/the-echoes-are-wide-awake.
90   He had come to . . . just called him "fat.": Underwood, "The Echoes Are Wide Awake."
90   The pressure doesn't scare me.: Underwood, "The Echoes Are Wide Awake."
91   Cornerback Bennett Jackson said, "Everybody . . . three minutes and 16 seconds: Matt Fortuna,
      "Notre Dame, Stanford Remember 2012," *ESPN.com*, Oct. 2, 2014, http://www.espn.go.com/
      college-football/story/_/id/11626627/notre-dame-fighting-irish-stanford-cardinal-remember-
      goal-line-stand-2012.
91   I was still celebrating. I was gonna celebrate until that call was made.: Fortuna, "Notre Dame,
      Stanford, Remember 2012."
92   "beautiful basketball" that was like "a lightning strike.": Brian Hartnett, "Notre Dame Storms by
      North Carolina," *The Observer*, March 17, 2015, http://ndsmcobserver.com/2015/03/notre-
      dame-storms-north-carolina-win-acc-championship-game/.
92   For one weekend, Notre Dame finalized its arrival in the ACC.: Mike Monaco, "Notre Dame
      Finalizes Its ACC Arrival," *The Observer*, March 17, 2015, http://ncsmcobserver.com/2015/03/
      monaco-notre-dame-finalizes-acc-arrival.
93   Leahy sought and received . . . hours and hours.": Heisler, *"Then Ara Said to Joe . . .", p. 23.
93   Bertilli was overwhelmed by calling the plays and the signals and then executing.: Heisler, *Then
      Ara Said to Joe . . .", p. 24.
93   The head coach "was . . . to concentrate on passing.: Heisler, *Then Ara Said to Joe . . .", p. 24.
93   It was all brand-new to us.: Heisler, *Then Ara Said to Joe . . .", p. 24.
94   "is considered to be . . . time they played them.: ""1988 Notre Dame Fighting Irish Football Team,"
      Wikipedia, the free encyclopedia, http://en.wikipedia.org/wiki/1988_Notre_Dame_Fighting_
      Irish_football_team.
94   With plans of becoming . . . whole bunch of A's.: Jake Kaplan, "Ho Has Fond Memories," philly.com,
      Jan. 4, 2013, http://articles.philly.com/2013-01-04/sports/36132811_1_notre-dame-stadium-
      manti-te-o-bcs-championship.
94   "a nerd who studies too much.": Barca, *Unbeatable*, p. 101.
94   by far the team's smallest player.: "Reginald Ho," *Wikipedia, the free encyclopedia*, http://en.
      wikipedia.org/wiki/Reginald_ho.
94   TV announcer Pat Haden said he had to get his jersey in the bookstore.: Barca, *Unbeatable*, p. 101.
94   Ho would line up behind . . . before driving the ball.: Kaplan, "Ho Has Fond Memories.
94   Haden called it "this voodoo or this kung-fu routine of his.": Barca, *Unbeatable*, p. 101.
94   Even Ho's brother, Tim, said it looked silly.: Kaplan, "Ho Has Fond Memories."
94   Going 4-for-4 against . . . of became a folk hero, really.: Kaplan, "Ho Has Fond Memories."
95   After the 14-6 win . . the Notre Dame head coach.: Garner, *et al, Echoes of Notre Dame Football*, p. 80.
95   Parseghian "was just worn out": Garner, *et al, Echoes of Notre Dame Football*, p. 79.
95   He was taking sleeping pills . . . before making his decision public.: Garner, *et al, Echoes of Notre
      Dame Football*, p. 80.
95   "they didn't owe me . . . play a great game.": Garner, *et al, Echoes of Notre Dame Football*, p. 80.
95   "It was the biggest play I ever made,": Garner, *et al, Echoes of Notre Dame Football*, p. 81.
95   That was a much more pleasant way of leaving the game.: Garner, *et al, Echoes
      of Notre Dame Football*, p. 81.

WORKS CITED

"1988 Notre Dame Fighting Irish Football Team." *Wikipedia, the free encylopedia.* http://en. wikipedia.org/wiki/1988_Notre_Dame_Fighting_Irish_football_team.

"Angelo Bertelli." UHND.com. http://www.uhnd.com/history/heismans/angelo-bertelli.

Arnold, Keith. "Catching Up with . . . Shane Arnold." *Inside the Irish.* 24 Sept. 2009. http://irish. nbcsports.com/2009/09/24/catching-up-with-shane-walton/.

-----. "Irish Memories: Reggie Brooks and the Snow Bowl." *NBC Sports.* 17 March 2011. http://irish. nbcsports.com/2011/03/17/irish-memories-reggie-brooks-and-the-snow-bowl/.

Ballard, Chris. "She's a Kick." *SI.com.* 17 Nov. 2003. http://www.si.com/vault/2013/11/17/354132/ she's-a-kick.

Barca, Jerry. "Notre Dame-Miami Rivalry Dominated College Football Landscape." *UND.com.* 5 Oct. 2012. http://www.und.com/genrel/100512aae.html.

-----. *Unbeatable: Notre Dame's 1988 Championship and the Last Great College Football Season.* New York: St. Martin's Griffin, 2013.

Bettinger, Jim & Julie S. *The Book of Bowden.* Nashville: TowleHouse Publishing, 2001.

Bourret, Tim. "Digger Phelps and Notre Dame: A Dream Realized." *UND.COM.* 18 Jan. 2014. http://www.und.com/sports/m-baskbl/spec-rel/011814aaa.html.

Brey Coached Despite Mother's Death." *ESPN.go.com.* 24 March 2015. http://espn.go.com/mens-college-basketball/tournament/2015/story/_/id/12548987/notre-dame-coach-mike-brey-never-considered-missing-game.

Briggs, David. "Golden Opportunity." *The Blade.* 20 Dec. 2015. http://www.bcsn.tv/news_article/show/591298.

Brown, Dennis. "Alumna Haley Scott DeMaria to Deliver 2012 Notre Dame Commencement Address." *Notre Dame News.* 28 March 2012. http://news.nd.edu/news/29908-alumna-haley-scott-demaria-to-deliver-2012-notre-dame-commencement-address/.

Burlage, Todd. "A Twist of Fate Leads Sanford Through Coaching Ranks." UND.com. 19 Oct. 2015. http://www.und.com/sports/m-footbl/spec-rel/10195aae.html.

-----. "Frank Leahy: A Coach for Two Schools." *UND.com.* 17 Nov. 2015. http://www.und.com/sports/m-footbl/spec-rel/111715aaa.html.

-----. "Overcoming the Odds." *UND.com.* 29 Aug. 2014. http://www.und.com/sports/m-footbl/spec-rel/082914aad.html.

-----. "Prosise's Journey: From Good to Great." *UND.com.* 10 Dec. 2015. http://wwww.und.com/sports/m-footbl/spec-rel/121015aac.html.

Burns, Marty. "Lyron Cobbins." *SI.com.* 1 Aug. 1996. http://www.si.com/vault/1996/08/01/216918/lyron-cobbins.

"Bus Crash Survivors [sic] Offers Hope to Others." *ESPN.go.com.* 5 June 2008. http://sports.espn.go.com/ espn/wire?id=3428054.

Carson, Alex. "Prosise Runs His Way into Notre Dame Record Books." *The Observer.* 22 Sept. 2015. http://ndsmcobserver.com/2015/09/football-teleconference-wrap/.

Condon, David. "Life Is a Party for Czarobski." *Chicago Tribune.* 15 Sept. 1977. http://www.archives.chicagotribune.com/1977/09/15/page/58/article/life-is-a-party-for-czarobski.

Coyne, Tom. "Notre Dame Linebacker Joe Schmidt Goes from Walk-On to Captain." *MSN.com.* 8 Oct. 2015. http://www.msn.com/en-us/sports/ncaafb/notre-dame-linebacker-schmidt-goes-from-walk-on-to-captain/ar-AAffRdg?ocid=U221DHP.

Daly, Sarah E. "For the 16,0000th Time . . . ." *UND.com.* 8 Oct. 2004. http://www.und.com/genrel/100804aaa.html.

DeFranks, Matthew. "Shane Walton Moves from Soccer to Coaching." *The Observer.* 26 Sept. 2013. http://www.ndmscobserver.com/2013/09/shane-walton-moves-from-soccer-to-coaching/.

Deitsch, Richard. "Win One for the Home Team." *Sports Illustrated.* 14 Nov. 2011. http://www.si.com/vault/2011/11/14/106130688/win-one-for-the-home-team.

Dent, Jim. *Resurrection: The Miracle Season That Saved Notre Dame.* New York City: St. Martin's Press, 2009.

Doyle, Joseph. *Fighting Irish: A Century of Notre Dame Football.* Charlottesville, Va.: Howell Press, 1987.

Fineran, John. "Notre Dame Squeaks by South Carolina to Secure Spot in NCAA Title Game." *South Bend Tribune.* 6 April 2015. http://www.ndinsider.com/basketball/womens/notre-dame-squeaks-by-south-carolina-to-secure-spot-in/article.

Fortuna, Matt. "Irish Deliver Final Blow in Michigan Rivalry." *ESPN.com*. 7 Sept. 2014. http://www.espn.go.com/blog/ncfnation/post/_/id/98314-irish-deliver-final-blow-in-michigan-rivalry.

-----. "Notre Dame, Stanford Remember 2012." *ESPN.com*. 2 Oct. 2014, http://www.espn.go.com/college-football/story/_/id/11626627/notre-dame-fighting-irish-stanford-cardinal-remember-goal-line-stand-2012.

"Frank Leahy." *Wikipedia, the free encyclopedia*. https://en.wikipedia.org/wiki/Frank_Leahy.

Frank, Mike. "Just to Be on the Team." *Scout.com*. 7 July 2005. http://www.scout.com/college/notre-dame/story/393489-just-to-be-on-the-team.

Game Day: Notre Dame Football. Chicago: Triumph Books, 2006.

Garner, Joe, Regis Philbin, Ara Paraseghian, and Joe Theismann. *Echoes of Notre Dame Football: Great and Memorable Moments of the Fighting Irish*. Naperville, Ill.: Sourcebooks, Inc., 2001.

Gildea, William and Christopher Jennison. *The Fighting Irish: Notre Dame Football Through the Years*. Englewood Cliffs, N.J.: Prentice-Hall, Inc., 1976.

Goodwin, Janelle. "Defying Diagnosis, Notre Dame Alum Walks and Swims Again After Crash." *CatholicPhilly.com*. 30 Oct. 2015. http://catholicphilly.com/2015/10/news/local-news/defying-diagnosis-swimmer-walks-and-swims-again-after-horrific-crash/.

Green, Mary. "Split-QB Game Plan Leads to Irish Victory." *The Observer*. 30 Dec. 2014. http://www.ndsmcobserver.com/2014/12/split-qb-game-plan-leads-to-irish-victory.

Greenberg, Jon. "Touting Trophy's Only All-Chicago Winner." *ESPN.go.com*. 28 Oct. 2011. http://espn.go.com/chicago/ncf/story/_/page/heisman-chicago-week2/john-lattner.

Hansen, Eric. "Backup Quarterback Deshone Kizer Helps Notre Dame Sidestep Upset." *ND Insider.com*. 12 Sept. 2015. http://www.ndinsider.com/fooball/backup-quarterback-deshone-kizer-helps-notre-dame-sidestep-upset/article_4d0ad9ca-59be-11e5-8be4-6314847bcf9.html.

-----. *Stadium Stories: Notre Dame Fighting Irish*. Guilford, Conn.: The Globe Pequot Press, 2004.

Hardie, Ann. "Being Skylar Diggins." *Notre Dame Magazine*. Winter 2012-13. http://magazine.nd.edu/news/36628-being-skylar-diggins/

Hartnett, Brian. "Notre Dame Storms by North Carolina to Win ACC Championship Game." *The Observer*. 17 March 2015. http://ndsmcobserver.com/2015/03/notre-dame-storms-north-carolina-win-acc-championship-game/.

Hays, Graham. "Diggins 'Owns the Day' in Record Win." *espnW.com*. 31 March 2013. http://espn.go.com/womens-college-basketball/tournament/2013/story/_-id/9117457/womens-ncaa-tournament-2013-skylar-diggins-hoops-mastery-record-setting-game.

Heinen, Devon. "Saving Best for Last at Notre Dame." *ESPN.go.com*. 23 April 2013. http://espn.go.com/lacrosse/story/_id/9185534/lacrosse-notre-dame-goalie-john-kemp-carries-family-tradition.

Heisler, John. *Greatest Moments in Notre Dame Football History*. Chicago: Triumph Books, 2008.

-----. "Sunday Brunch: Nobody Better at Home." *UND.com*. 15 Nov. 2015. http://www.und.com/sports/m-footbl/spec-rel/111515aaa.html.

-----. *"Then Ara Said to Joe. . .": The Best Notre Dame Football Stories Ever Told*. Chicago: Triumph Books, 2007.

Hettler, Joe. "Pruzinsky Wins Big East Honors." *The Observer*. 20 Feb. 2004. http://www.ndsmcobserver.com/2004/02/pruzinsky-wins-big-east-honors.

Hine, Chris. "Cohesive Quarterback Tandem Works for Notre Dame in Music City Bowl." *Chicago Tribune*. 30 Dec. 2014. http://www.chicagotribune.com/sports/college/ct-notre-dame-lsu-football-spt-1231-20141230-story.html.

Ismail. "The Green Machine: A History of Notre Dame's Green Jerseys." *BleacherReport.com*. 9 March 2010. http://www.bleacherreport.com/articles/359516-the-green-machine-a-history-of-notre-dames-green-jerseys.

Jackson, Scoop. "The Skylar Diggins Balancing Act." *ESPN.go.com*. 23 Dec. 2011. http://espn.go.com/espn/commentary/story/_./page/jackson-111223/skylar-diggins-notre-dame-balances-beauty-athleticism.

Jennings, Chantel. "Linked History Preserves a Rivalry." *ESPN.go.com*. 6 Sept. 2013. http://www.espn.go.com/college-football/story/_/id/9640386/the-historic-notre-dame-michigan-rivalry-never-really-gone.

Kaplan, Jake. "Ho Has Fond Memories of Notre Dame's 1988 Championship Season." *philly.com*. 4 Jan. 2013, http://articles.philly.com/2013-01-04/sports/36132811_1_notre-dame-stadium-manti-te-o-bcs-

NOTRE DAME

championship.

Kissane, John A. "Molly Seidel: 'I've Been Hearing about That Stupid Curse for Years.'" *Runners World.com*. 24 Nov. 2015. http://www.runnersworld.com/college/molly-seidel-ive-been-hearing-about-that-stupid-curse-for-years.

Kollars, Bob. "Joe Schmidt and the Spirit of Notre Dame." *UHND.com*. 16 June 2013. http://www.uhnd.com/articles/football/spirit-notre-dame.

Kruvant, Mackenzie. "18 Things You Should Actually Know about Skylar Diggins." *BuzzFeed*. 17 July 2014. http://www.buzzfeed.com/mackenziekruvant/things-you-should-actually-know-about-skylar-diggins#.xfgAYPdZKA.

LaFleur, Pete. "Andrea McHugh: Freedom Through Faith, Both On and Off the Court." *UND.com*. 5 Nov. 2013. http://www.und.com/sports/w-volley/spec-rel/110513aae.html.

-----. "Celebrating 25 Years of Excellence." *UND.com*. 18 Oct. 2012. http://www.und.com/sports/w-soccer/spec-rel/101812aaa.html.

Layden, Tim. "Modern Irish." *SI.com*. 26 Nov. 2012. http://www.si.com/vault/2012/11/26/106258863/modern-irish.

"Leon Hart." *UHND.com*. http://www.uhnd.com/history/heismans/leon-hart/.

"Leon Lifts #7/10 Notre Dame to NCAA Title in 1-0 Win over #1/1 Stanford." *UND.com*. 5 Dec. 2010. http://www.und.com/sports/w-soccer/recaps/120510aaa.html.

Lesar, Al. "Notre Dame's Unlikely Heroes Embrace Moment in Final Four Win." *South Bend Tribune*. 5 April 2015. http://www.ndinsider.com/basketball/womens/notre-dame-s-unlikely-heroes-embrace-moment-in-final-four/article.

Mandel, Stewart. "Show Stopper." *Sports Illustrated*. 20 Sept. 2004. http://www.si.com/vault/2004/09/20/8185824/show-stopper.

McDermott, Barry. "After 88 Comes Zero." *SI.com*. 28 Jan. 1974. http://www.si.com/vault/1974/01/28/617039/after-88-comes-zero.

Monaco, Mike. "Notre Dame Finalizes Its ACC Arrival." *The Observer*. 17 March 2015. http://ncsmcobserver.com/2015/03/monaco-notre-dame-finalizes-acc-arrival.

-----. "Waking the Echoes: Darius Walker." *The Observer*. 25 Sept. 2014. http://ndsmcobserver.com/2014/09/waking-echoes-darius-walker/.

Murphy, Austin. "Round 1 to the Irish: Notre Dame Upset Florida State in a Nail-Biter." *SI.com*. 22 Nov. 1993. http://www.si.com/vault/1993/11/22/129948/round-1-to-the-irish.

Myslenski, Skip. "Notre Dame Goes Kicking into the Cotton." *SI.com*. 30 Nov. 1970. http://www.si.com/vault/1970/11/30/611874/notre-dame-goes-kicking-into-the-cotton.

"Navy-Notre Dame Football Rivalry." *Wikipedia, the free encyclopedia*. http://en.wikipedia.org/wiki/Navy-Notre-Dame_football_rivalry.

"NCAA Championship Game Postgame Quotes." *UND.com*. 5 Dec. 2010. http://www.und.com/sports/w-soccer/recdas/120510aaf.html.

Newman, Bruce. "The Master of Disaster Kelly Tripucka Grew Up Scuffling with His Five Brothers." *Sports Illustrated*. 19 Jan. 1981. http://www.si.com/vault/1981/01/19/825294/the-master-of-disaster.

"Notre Dame Fencing Springs from Modest Beginnings to National Prominence." http://publish.netitor.com/photos/schools/nd/sport/c-fenc/auto_pdf/fencing-history.pdf.

"Notre Dame Rallies to Outlast Upset-Minded Pitt in Triple Overtime." *ESPN*. 4 Nov. 2012. http://scores.espn.go.com/ncf/recap?gameId=323080087.

"Notre Dame-USC Football Rivalry." *Wikipedia, the free encylopedia*. https://en.wikipedia.org/wiki/Notre_Dame-USC_football_rivalry.

"Notre Dame Victory March." *UND.com*. http://www.und.com/trads/nd-fightsong.html.

"Notre Dame vs. Syracuse, 11/18/1961." *University of Notre Dame Archives*. www.archives.nd.edu/about/news/index.php/2011/nd-vs-syracuse-11181961/#.VEAfVPnF-So.

"November 14, 1992 — The Snow Bowl." *TodayinNDHistory.com*. http://www.todayinndhistory.com/pages/events/?id=391.

Patel, Avani. "When Joe Recendez Learned He Needed Surgery for Testicular Cancer, It Just Meant the Notre Dame Tight End Had to Work Even Harder to Get Back on the Field." *Chicago Tribune*. 8 Nov. 2000. http://articles.chicagotribune.com/2000-11-08/sports/0011080164_1_testicular-cancer-notre-dame-surgery.

Patrick, Dick. "Riley Ends Notre Dame Career with Title." *USA Today*. 2 April 2001. http://usatoday30.usatoday.com/sports/basketball/marchmania/2001/womens/stories/2001-04-01-riley-finale.htm#more.

"Paul Hornung." *UHND.com*. http://uhnd.com/history/heismans/paul-hornung.

Phelps, Digger with Tom Bourret. *Digger Phelps's Tales from the Notre Dame Hardwood*. Champaign, Ill.: Sports Publishing L.L.C, 2004.

"Postcard Views of Notre Dame." *IrishLegends.com*. http://www.irishlegends.com/Pages/postcard/postcard_nov01.htm. The material on the website is lifted from *The University of Notre Dame: A Portrait of Its History and Campus* by Thomas Schlereth.

Prister, Tim, ed. *What It Means to Be Fighting Irish*. Chicago: Triumph Books, 2004.

Rallo, Curt. "Jarrett Grace's Long Road to Recovery." *UND.com*. 15 April 2015. http://www.und.com/sports/m-footbl/spec-rel/041515aaa.html.

-----. "Jewell's Drive." *UND.com*. 17 march 2015. http://www.und.com/sports/w-baskbl/spec-rel/031715aaa.html.

-----. "Ossello Flips the Switch to Football." *UND.com*. 28 Oct. 2015. http://www.und.com/sports/m-footbl/spec-rel/102815aad.html.

Reed, William F. "Lee Becton: Cotton." *Sports Illustrated*. 10 Jan. 1994. http://www.si.com/vault/1994/01/10/130229/lee-becton-cotton.

"Reginald Ho." *Wikipedia, the free encyclopedia*. http://en.wikipedia.org/wiki/Reginald_Ho.

"Rick Mirer." *Wikipedia, the free encyclopedia*. http://en.wikipedia.org/wiki/Rick_Mirer.

Rodio, Michael. "More Than a Game." *Notre Dame Magazine*. Summer 2012. http://magazine.nd.edu/news/31345/more-than-a-game.

"Ruth Riley." *Wikipedia, the free encyclopedia*. http://en.wikipedia.org/wiki/Ruth_Riley.

Somogyi, Lou. "Austin Carr Enters The Ring." *notredame247sports.com*. 26 Feb. 2011. http://notredame.247sports.com/Article/Austin-Carr-Notre Dames-Greatest-Ever-In-Basketball-16497.

-----. "The Ties That Bind: Navy Truly Kept Notre Dame Afloat During World War II." *UND.com*. 27 Oct. 2011. http://www.UND.com/sports/m-footbl/spec-rel/102711aah.html?wappref=std.

Stankevitz, J.J. "Finally Pain Free, Jarrett Grace Ready to Return for Notre Dame." *CSNCHICAGO.com*. 16 Aug. 2015. http://www.csnchicago.com/notre-dame-finally-ready-return-notre-dame.

Staples, Andy. "For Notre Dame's Tuitt, Path to BCS Began on Georgia Road." *SI.com*. 2 Jan. 2013. http://sportsillustrated.cnn.com/college-football/news/20130102/stephon-truitt-notre-dame.

"Sweet 61: Carr's Tourney Scoring Record Stands Test of Time." *UND.com*. 26 March 2015. http://www.und.com/sports/m-baskbl/spec-real/032615aaf.html

Swindoll, Charles. "Analysis of a Courtroom Fiasco." *Sermon Series: Jesus: The Greatest Life of All*. http://daily. insight.org/site/News2?page=NewsArticle&id=9653.

Thamel, Pete. "Notre Dame's Rout of Texas Confirms Irish Are Better with Malik Zaire at QB." *SI.com*. 6 Sept. 2015. http://www.si.com/college-football/2015/09/06-notre-dame-fighting-irish-texas-longhorns-malik-zaire.

Thomas, Laura. "Nick Ossello: Notre Dame Renaissance Man." *UND.com*. 22 Sept. 2015. http://www.und.com/blog/2015/09/nick-ossello-notre-dame-renaissance-man.html.

Tybor, Joseph. "Anthony Johnson Quietly Punches Up Notre Dame Offense." *Chicago Tribune*. 27 Sept. 1989. http://www.articles.chicagotribune.com/1989-09-27/sports/8901170654_1_irish-offense-purdue-coach-fred-akers-notre-dame.

Underwood, John. "The Echoes Are Wide Awake." *Sports Illustrated*. 29 Sept. 1975. http://www.si.com/vault/1975/09/29/606783/the-echoes-are-wide-awake.

Vorel, Mike. "Despite Position Change, Carlyle Holiday Still Owns QB Mentality." *South Bend Tribune*. 3 Aug. 2015. http://www.ndinsider.com/football/despite-position-change-and-career-move-carlyle-holiday-still-owns/article_6929ea26-3a27-11e5-8455-bbe89d-f3291e.html.

Winn, Luke. "Going Gaga for 'Gody." *SI.com*. 17 March 2008. http://www.si.com/vault/2008/03/17/104581281/going-gag-for-gody.

Zimmerman, Paul. "The Golden Boys After World War II." *Sports Illustrated*. 24 Nov. 1997. http://www.si.com/vault/1997/11/24/235251/the-golden-boys-after-world- war-ii.

Zuba, Samantha. "Unfinished Business: Joe Schmidt." *The Observer*. 20 Nov. 2014. http://www.ndsmcobserver.com/2014/11/unfinished-business-joe-schmidt.

NAME INDEX
(LAST NAME, DEVOTION DAY NUMBER)

207

SCRIPTURES INDEX
(by DEVOTION DAY NUMBER)

FIGHTING IRISH